THE
SENSEI
LEADER

Jim Bouchard

San Chi Publishing
2015

To Alexandra Armstrong—

Here's to the start of our next adventure. I love you and—
Thank You!

To Christopher Keith—

Chris is not only one of my dearest friends, but without his
generosity and commitment this book would not be a reality.

As editor, Chris helped craft the words of this book.

More important—as my brother in the arts and my
colleague throughout my martial arts career, Chris
helped shape the Sensei who wrote this book.

You've been my treasured teacher, mentor and
advocate in the dojo—and in life.

This one's for you.

This book is also dedicated to the Men and Women
who serve in our military, police and fire services—

You are the true warriors.

Thank You for Your Service.

"Jim Bouchard nails it with this refreshing, vibrant book about leadership."

While he outlines the essential qualities of leadership: *courage, compassion, character*—his thrust is that being a good leader is not just about leading, but about imparting leader qualities to subordinates so leadership at all levels within an organization can take root and flourish.

Using the teachings, techniques , and philosophies of martial arts, Jim explores—and explains—how the old adage "leaders are born, not made" is simply not so. Leadership, he insists, can and should be taught, and can and should be learned. It is, he points out, "... not only *possible* at all levels but a *responsibility* at all levels".

Recalling from his own experiences, Jim asserts that anyone who really wants to become a leader can if he, or she, is willing to try. An important part of that process is the mentor, or *Sensei*.

"The Sensei Leader is a great way to begin the teaching process, and is perfect for those in leadership positions who want to build a bench of good leaders at all levels within their organization."

ADMIRAL LEIGHTON "SNUFFY" SMITH
USN, Retired

Jim Bouchard shows us how to unshackle, release, and become the leader we aspire to be in *The Sensei Leader.*

"If you want to be a more effective leader, read this book and diligently apply its lessons. Both you and the people you want to influence will be much, much better for it."

RANDY PENNINGTON
Author of **Make Change Work**
Pennington Performance Group
www.penningtongroup.com

Jim Bouchard has a remarkable way of relating his own personal experiences of challenge, awakening and growth to the reader in a way that transmits a "how-to" for self-motivation and leadership development.

"Drawing upon Jim's personal testimony, **The Sensei Leader** *takes hard-learned lessons from the grit and hard-knocks of the Dojo and sends a knock-out punch of personal responsibility to the reader."*

His key message: *"Listen More, Learn More, Fear Less!"* resonates as a wake-up call to developing and established leaders to engage at all levels, and grow from within to become the Sensei.

It is obvious that Jim has poured his spirit and personal story into this Leadership handbook!

COLONEL MATTHEW T. FRITZ

Co-Founder and Senior Curator of GeneralLeadership.com
The General Leadership Foundation
GeneralLeadership.com

"Jim Bouchard's **The Sensei Leader** *is about mastering the disciplines to discover the true that leader that resides in all of us."*

Bouchard's Sensei approach puts one's own thinking and behavior under the microscope, breaks it down, and incrementally reconditions it until a worthy leader emerges. Bouchard expertly weaves his own journey from self-destruction to his pivotal transformational moment to lead himself in order to lead others.

"Bouchard's **The Sensei Leader** *dives deep into the thinking and behavior that every leader must explore and master."*

NEIL DUCOFF

Founder & CEO of Strategies
Author of the award-winning book *No-Compromise Leadership*

"We are all leaders at some point in our lives ..."

We might lead families, businesses, sports teams, charity events, social circles, book clubs, or students.

We all need to read *The Sensei Leader*. This book is touching, enlightening, provocative, and most of all practical. It also garners together a plethora of insightful quotes from iconic leaders you will want to memorize.

"Practical books on leadership are rare, but this book delivers. It has deep, insightful observations on the real ingredients of great leadership: confidence, generosity, focus, mindfulness, humility, courage and many more."

IAN D. SMITH

Ex CFO, CEO, Investment Banker, VC, World Class Masters Track Guy
and Author of **The Smith Report Blog**
PortfolioPartnership.com/blog

"All present and future leaders should read and re-read this book. It will challenge your leadership instincts and transform you into a true Sensei Leader*. "*

The Sensei Leader outlines a clear path for leadership within the Sensei tradition.

Many have discussed what being a Sensei truly means but it is Bouchard who reminds us that Sensei literally means *"one who went before."* With this as his foundation, he instructs us with a real world, practical guide to leadership.

By presenting a continual learning voyage model, he utilizes the Sensei philosophy of helping others to reach their full potential as well as giving service to one's followers. Through this process, we can all truly become leaders in today's fast-paced world.

DR. JOHN TANTILLO

The Marketing Doctor
Branding Editor, *Fridge Magazine*, Branding and Marketing Expert

*"**The Sensei Leader** is told on several levels: From kid to Adult! From drug addiction to Sensei! From loser to Leader!"*

The book is a mirror, an eye opening melt into how martial arts principles can be applied in today's leadership to achieve an agent for transformation.

... substance for deep thought as there are some truly remarkable gems from real life experiences to pick from this book.

"Sparkling!"

JARO BERCE

Author of **Leadership by Virtue**
LeadershipbyVirtue.blogspot.com

*"**The Sensei Leader** masterfully weaves personal experiences with sound, fundamental leadership principles."*

This will be a great read for anyone interested in the pursuit of leadership. These messages will find a special place in the hearts of those traveling a non-traditional leadership path.

EARL BREON

Layman Leadership Blog

"Jim Bouchard has a unique ability to take a complex subject like leadership and make it simple to master."

The Sensei Leader will help you fulfill your purpose while helping your people reach their full potential. It is required reading for new leaders and the book experienced leaders will wish they had sooner.

GEORGE KRUEGER & MARY-LYNN FOSTER

Co-Founders, BIGG Success
BiggSuccess.com

"I love this book!

Real leadership from someone with the experience of what it takes to be at the top of your game. Someone who has had the courage to turn things around, someone who has the compassion to give others the very best of himself, someone with the wisdom of a Black Belt.

Jim says "leaders are carved from experience" this book is carved from the very best!

ROWDY MCLEAN

Speaker and Author of *Play a Bigger Game*

"Jim Bouchard has done a extraordinary job in guiding us to the truth; that the real power of leadership is not a force of will, but rather, an ongoing process of honoring and respecting all parties."

So rarely does a leadership expert grasp the power and the marriage of compassion and courage the way Jim does.

"Jim is The Sensei of Leadership because his approach to leadership development is both poised and clearly on point for those who can grasp that business, like the dojo, must be a sacred space where all are called to step into their greatness!"

DOV BARON

Speaker and author of *Fiercely Loyal*

CONTENTS

i

PART TWO
THE ESSENTIAL CHARACTERISTICS OF THE SENSEI LEADER

PART THREE
STRATEGIES AND TACTICS

PART FOUR

THE SPIRIT OF THE SENSEI LEADER

FOREWORD

This is a great book. A really great book ...

But I'm not going to tell you about the book. I'm going to tell you about the author, Jim Bouchard. In doing so I can assure you that you'll get insights about what's in the book.

I first met Jim when he was a student in a weekend seminar on professional speaking that I was co-teaching. Jim was just getting started in the business, and what immediately impressed me was that he came to our seminar with a true "Beginner's Mind." It was obvious that he was there to learn.

In a room full of big personalities and even bigger egos, Jim had checked his ego at the door. His interest was in getting better, not in making an impression. And, in having that attitude, he made a very positive impression on my teaching partner and me.

Over the months following the seminar, we stayed in touch

with Jim and closely followed his progress. What became quickly apparent was something remarkable—Jim was taking all of the ideas we discussed and actually putting them into practice.

He was doing the work. This wasn't quick return, instant gratification work. This was nose to the grindstone work. It was go out and hit it again day after day work.

You'll see in the book that Jim talks about his early experience in the dojo, when his teacher praised him for "staying in there" and for "standing your ground."

Jim came back day after day, putting into practice those practices that we had taught him would work, but only if done with patience and consistency. This was our first indication of the core leadership qualities that I have since observed that Jim has in him right down to his bones.

I'll let you read the book for yourself, but let me share a little of my perspective about this book with you.

I've been working with business leaders for over thirty years. I've had the great privilege of learning from some of the best, and I've worked to discover and pass along the essence of the qualities of effective leadership.

Jim has a unique approach, revealing best leadership practices through the lens of *The Sensei Leader*. I know little about martial arts, but from this book I discover that there is no better model for developing true leadership skills.

What makes this book particularly useful is that, whether you've ever been exposed to martial arts or not, you will quickly discover that this book is about *you*. It's about your life. It's about your leadership challenges and opportunities.

The lessons in *The Sensei Leader* apply to the range of human experience, and the principles apply to every leader in every kind of organization.

Finally, what is most meaningful to me about *The Sensei Leader* is that it is ultimately about *courage, compassion,* and *wisdom.*

In this book you'll learn of the courage that Jim has brought to the challenges of his own life. Through his words you'll get a sense of the great compassion that this man carries in his heart and soul. In every chapter, in every paragraph, you'll benefit from the wisdom that Jim has acquired through his own life lessons, and that he so generously shares in the pages of this book.

I'm happy for you that you've got this book. It will cause you to think about your role, your potential, and your promise as a leader in ways that you never have before.

What I really hope for you, though, is that some day you get to meet Jim Bouchard face to face. I hope that you get to experience his courage, compassion, and wisdom in person. That experience is something you will always remember, and always treasure.

Jim Bouchard was my student.

The student ... has become my teacher.

Joe Calloway
Author of **Be Your Best at What Matters Most**
and **Becoming a Category of One**

JoeCalloway.com

PREFACE

This book is not a book about solutions. My sole intention is to share my ideas and experiences—my hope is to instigate some thought and discussion.

Some of my perspectives may challenge your concept of what a "leader" is. That's OK—let's debate and see what comes of it.

Some of my ideas may simply validate yours. That's OK too—sometimes validation is just as valuable as education.

The problem with a book is that it's only one part of the conversation. That's why I speak and do workshops and training for businesses. That's where we can really dig in, discuss the issues and see how to best put these ideas to work for you, your organization, and your people.

I will state for the record that I prefer to work with organizations that already have a strong leadership culture. I can't fix bad. I can help you make a good culture even better—or keep a great culture going strong.

We produce real results when I work with leaders who fully embrace the idea that *perfection is not a destination, it's a never-ending process*—a theme you're going to hear throughout this book.

A quick note:
I write with the masculine pronoun because I am a man.

It seems strange to me that this even needs to be said, but I want to state clearly that in the dojo, in life and certainly in the world of leadership, women and men are fully equal.

I just find it awkward and distracting when a writer bounces back and forth between feminine and masculine pronouns or worse—writes in the complimentary gender in some vain attempt to appear politically correct or erudite.

So—for the record—leaders are not exclusively men or women.

Leaders are *people.*

I do my best to stay focused on the human side of leadership. To this end, I share a lot of my personal life—adventures—and misadventures.

I believe strongly that leadership is about transformation. My hope is that my own transformation shows, from the heart, that if I could do it—so can you.

I do my best to reinforce the idea that true leaders exist at all levels—and should be cultivated at all levels.

Every one of us has the capability to be an authentic leader. Leadership has nothing to do with rank, title or position—it has nothing to do with degrees or certificates.

Leadership is—above all—our willingness to live as an example to others.

It is our deepest expression of our commitment to other human beings.

It is a full acceptance of our responsibility to the people we share our lives with and an understanding of our part in the community of humankind.

Simple—not easy!

"THE BENEVOLENT MAN REAPS THE BENEFIT ONLY AFTER OVERCOMING DIFFICULTIES."

~CONFUCIUS

INTRODUCTION

A leader's most important tool—a mirror.

That's right—a mirror.

A martial artist spends a lot of time in front of the mirror. Leaders should spend a lot of time in front of the mirror too.

Most dojos have a wall of mirrors. This isn't to check out how pretty you are—it's so you can see the flaws in your technique. Sure, it's nice when you catch a glimpse of yourself during a moment of brilliance, but for every one of those moments, there are hundreds of hours of hard work, struggle and failure.

THE DOJO STAIRS

The first time I set foot in a dojo was on a brisk spring day in 1985 ...

Walking up Congress Street, the main drag in Portland, Maine, I saw a gigantic sign hanging from the side of a building. K-A-R-A-T-E was spelled out in huge three foot letters. I walked up a long flight of stairs and saw two students throwing each other all over the floor. The dojo floor itself rose over the reception area up a wide set of stairs, the perfect stage to impress any aspiring student.

The floor was hollow underneath, so every time a body hit the floor, it produced a resounding boom. The scene had the intended effect. I was thoroughly impressed.

I was so impressed that I immediately turned around and walked right back down those stairs.

The instructor must have needed new students—he chased me down the stairs and into the street!

This man, Dick Roy, would become my first Sensei. I only knew him for a short time, but in that time he shared lessons that still inspire me today.

One story he told had to do with how you achieve your next rank, or any other goal for that matter. He set the story up by describing a series of step ladders. He said:

"You're standing on top of one ladder, but you want to get to the top of the next one. What do you have to do first?"

I thought this was pretty cool—here was one of those old fortune cookie stories I was hoping for from the wise master!

I thought about it for a while, but I really didn't have an answer.

"Climb down."

That story really went all the way in for me. Not because I was particularly ambitious about my next rank, but because it seemed to me that I spent most of my life, up to this point, falling off of ladders.

The reason I came to the dojo in the first place was to try and find a way to put my life in order. I was less than two years drug free at this point. For those who haven't had the experience, this may surprise you, but quitting drugs is easy. Staying off them is the hard part!

Instead of feeling good about life, I was stuck in a period of desperation and depression. I had very little money. My fiancée had just dumped me for another guy. I was living in a crappy little apartment with cardboard dressers and milk crate tables.

I was, once again, at the bottom of the ladder. I seriously considered suicide—and not for the first time. I was desperately afraid of how easy it would be to fall back into the comfort of drugs.

At some point you've probably cracked open a fortune cookie to see this pithy little philosophical tidbit:

"The journey of a thousand miles begins with a single step."

That wisdom comes from Lao Tzu and his *Tao Te Ching*. I can add, from experience, that the rest of the trip is a bunch of single steps, too.

Transformation is not a single moment. Transformation is a continual process made up of many steps along the way.

Some of those steps are forward, some are sideways and some even backward.

There are, however, some steps that stand out from the rest. There are certain moments that, with the benefit of hindsight anyway, distinguish themselves as important turning points. Many times, these are your lowest points, not your highest.

People often ask me about my turning point. They ask me for that one transcendent "moment of transformation" when I turned everything around. They're very often surprised to hear that starting martial arts was not my turning point.

That point came several months before I ever set foot in a dojo.

It involved a mirror, too.

STONEHENGE

It amazes me how often courage and desperation show up at the same time!

If it is courageous to quit drugs, I only acknowledge it in hindsight. I want to be very clear, I don't want to glamorize this part of my life in any way.

I don't think there's any great honor in quitting a self-destructive behavior like a drug addiction, and I don't like it when celebrities are applauded for the sole reason that they somehow didn't kill themselves.

True honor is found in doing the hard work necessary to create a productive and meaningful life.

Having said that, it does take courage to look in the mirror, face your worst self, and decide that something needs to change—and that something is you. I somehow found the courage to face what I had become when I was at my absolute worst.

I was living in an old 1950s vintage trailer near Sebago Lake in Maine. For those who don't know the area, it gets plenty cold there and this particular night, it was plenty cold!

This was one of those drafty old trailers with the heavy louvered glass windows. The wind was free to come and visit through any number of cracks and unfilled openings.

We tacked a sign over the door that read:

"We ARE the people our parents warned us about."

We christened our trailer, Stonehenge.

This is where I reached the lowest point in my life—and where I'd find the turning point.

Anyway, I went to bed that freezing night and pulled my sleeping bag up over my head to stay warm. We were running our "ghetto heat." That means we had run out of kerosene for the furnace, so we put a small electric fan in front of the open oven and hoped for the best.

Strange, but we somehow always had money for dope—but not for heat. Priorities, I suppose.

I woke up in the middle of the night, nature calling. Believe you me, I did not want to get out of my warm sleeping bag to take an inconvenient piss.

I couldn't stand it anymore! I jumped out of bed, stepped into the bathroom, and let go—only to realize that something didn't sound quite right.

I snapped on the light—there was a skim of ice frozen across the toilet.

I turned around to wash my hands and saw myself in the bathroom mirror. I just stood there for a while—staring into the mirror—disgusted.

How could I live this way? What was the point?

I looked hard at my face in that mirror and said, "This shit has got to stop. Now."

But nobody likes a quitter, right? I didn't quit drugs that night.

Not long after that I did quit. Not drugs—I quit college.

That's right, I was still in school at the time. After a terrific freshman year, I turned into a stoner. I earned a 3.8 GPA in my first year—now I was just like D-Day in the movie *Animal House,* I no longer had a grade point average—all classes incomplete.

I was so stupid and desperate at one point that I committed fraud by falsifying time sheets for my work/study program—all to keep the party going.

Speaking of parties—fast forward a few months to one of our infamous Stonehenge parties. These gatherings consisted of loud music, girls we didn't know, and plenty of people showing up willing to smoke our dope and pop our pills.

One redeeming factor, and probably the only one that kept me out of jail during this mess, was the fact that I never sold drugs. Of course, that only meant that every dime I made not only supported my habit, but also contributed to providing a good time for whoever else happened by. In some way I suppose that fed my need to be accepted and seen as one of the cool people.

Sometime during this party someone passed me a joint. I *Bogarted* said joint—for those unfamiliar with the term, this meant that refused to pass it along.

The plain fact is that I couldn't get off on just a joint. At that time, I was smoking 4 to 6 full bhang hits a day. I snorted speed to stay up and party and to get up for work in the morning. I popped Quaaludes and crossroads (Percocet) to mellow out and to counter the effects of the speed.

When I needed additional stimulation, I would try just about any pill anyone was willing to offer—and I would indulge in the occasional experiment with stronger hash or opium …

… but I was not a junky! At least that's what I told myself.

I staunchly refused to do cocaine or anything that involved a needle. To my mind, those were the drugs junkies did. I didn't snort blow or shoot smack—therefore, I was not a junky.

Anyway, despite the large quantities of marijuana I smoked, I was still generally a pretty mellow stoner. Not long after my last draw on this particular joint, I knew something wasn't quite right.

I started to get very agitated. From what I remember, I started running around the living room. I apparently tried to jump out through the heavy louvered glass window of our trailer.

Later I had a powerful craving for something to eat; you get the munchies when you're high, right?

(Careful, that's a trick question.)

I remember wanting to get into the refrigerator, but for some reason I thought I could stick my head right through the door. I must have bashed my head against the fridge four or five times before I gave up.

I can't remember the rest of the night.

What I do remember is walking into that bathroom the next morning and once again—there was that disgusting face in the mirror. I looked like I'd gone three rounds with Mike Tyson. I felt even worse than I looked.

That's when I quit. That is the exact moment when I finally decided enough was enough. In hindsight, that will have to serve as my transformational moment—my turning point.

That's when I knew that transformation was not optional. If I was going to survive, I needed to change.

By rights I should have been dead or in jail several times over. I didn't want to squander the opportunity I had to transform myself into a person I'd actually like to be—someone I might consider worthy of living.

Transformation is a powerful teacher. Self-transformation

may just be the most powerful and effective process to develop your full potential as a leader, provided that you're willing to embrace the full experience ...

... and you're willing to share.

There were plenty of challenges still ahead—many—many more steps, and at least a thousand miles ahead on this trip.

I didn't know it at the time, but learning how to face those challenges would shape who I would become as a person and as a leader.

My life as a martial artist and a Sensei has taught me one thing above all:

Perfection is not a destination. It's a never-ending process.

Sensei literally means *one who went before*. A leader is someone who is willing to walk point. Your job is to lead others through the never-ending process of change and transformation. That's what life is all about—that's what success and happiness are made out of.

In many ways, a leader is a mirror. Your followers see themselves in you—they want, in some small way, to be you or at least to be a part of you. It's your job to reflect back what your followers need to see to correct their flaws and improve themselves.

What do you see when you look in the mirror?

If you're going to lead others, you've first got to learn how to lead yourself. The first step on the thousand-mile journey is committing yourself to continual self-discovery, learning, growth and transformation.

Look in the mirror — a lot.

Take stock of who you are. Decide who you want to be. Before you turn that mirror on others, make sure you're comfortable with your own reflection.

Back to the dojo ...

PART ONE

THE MAKING OF A LEADER

A LEADER IS NOT BORN, OR MADE

I'm living proof that leaders are not born.

I'll take it a step further and say that leaders are not even made—they are transformed.

I certainly didn't follow the classic path to leadership.

I never held a C-suite job in a large corporation. I never served in the military—to this day my biggest regret. I never studied leadership in college.

I'm a two-time college dropout and former drug addict.

Terrific resume for a leader, right?

Given the choice, I wouldn't repeat my experiments in self-destruction, but now that I've made peace with my past life, I realize that being a loser was the perfect preparation for becoming a leader.

A LEADER IS AN AGENT FOR TRANSFORMATION

A leader transforms ideas into realities.

A leader transforms the potential of an individual into excellence in performance.

A leader transforms a group of individuals into a productive organization or community.

Your capacity to perform as an agent for transformation starts with you.

Before I could ever lead others, I had to lead myself out of what had become a crippling cycle of self-loathing, self-destruction, addiction and depression. You just can't transform others unless you know how to transform your Self.

First of all, leadership depends on credibility. If you're gonna talk the talk; you better walk the walk! If you're not sincere, if you don't know yourself, other people will see right through you. They will not trust you. If they don't trust you, they're not likely to follow you—at least not for long.

Any thug can control others with enough muscle—at least for a while. A genuine leader leads with true power, not by fear, force or coercion. I'll explain that in a while, but for now it's enough to acknowledge that true power comes from self-mastery, and ...

... all leadership starts with self-leadership.

So—before I could become a leader, my first job was to transform myself from loser to black belt.

Once I got my own life on track, I learned how to be a genuine leader through my service as a martial arts instructor—a Sensei.

By helping others transform and develop their true potential, I grew to understand my value as a human being and to get a sense of my potential as a leader. For me, this understanding came from helping other people become black belts. Anyone who understands martial arts can tell you that, done right, the black belt trip is not just about learning how to be a tough guy. It's about learning to be a leader by example.

Anyway—most of what I know about leadership comes from my 30 years and counting of study and practice in martial arts, and my 25 years and counting of experience as a Sensei, as a teacher.

The life of a Sensei, or of any teacher for that matter, is a life of service. You can only be effective as a teacher, or as a leader, by serving others—by helping other people reach their full potential.

Becoming a Sensei taught me the true meaning, power and influence of service in leadership.

Long ago—Lao Tzu wrote:

> "**ENLIGHTENED LEADERSHIP IS SERVICE, NOT SELFISHNESS. THE LEADER GROWS MORE AND LASTS LONGER BY PLACING THE WELL-BEING OF ALL ABOVE THE WELL-BEING OF SELF ALONE.**"

Like too many people, I didn't see myself as a leader at first—because I wasn't usually "the boss." Until I became a Sensei, I never really held any classic position of authority.

Frankly—I didn't think I was worthy.

After many painful years of bashing my head, figuratively and literally, I finally realized that leadership and authority are not always connected. Eventually, I learned that a true leader is really someone who is able to inspire other people to transform themselves into someone better, sometimes even better than they ever expected or imagined.

John Quincy Adams defined leadership this way:

> "**IF YOUR ACTIONS INSPIRE OTHERS TO DREAM MORE, LEARN MORE, DO MORE AND BECOME MORE, YOU ARE A LEADER.**"

You may be a leader and not even know it. Your thoughts, words and actions may inspire people far more than you realize, especially if you're a parent, coach, teacher. Your peers may see you as a leader, and your example may inspire them to "do more and become more" whether you realize it or not.

Once I became a Sensei, I realized that people were counting on me to be a leader whether I thought I was one or not. I came to realize that leadership was not optional. It was my responsibility.

I didn't always feel that way!

For most of my early adult life, I thought leadership was someone else's job. I definitely did not see myself as a leader. In many ways, I still considered myself a loser.

It took me a very long time to accept the responsibility of leadership and to embrace my identity as a leader.

THE IDEA OF A "LEADER" DEFINES A UNIQUELY HUMAN EXPERIENCE

Members of the herd, pack or flock don't follow a leader by conscious choice. They defer to the dominant member of the group. The leader of the pack is determined mostly by genetic traits like strength and fertility, and by age.

Intellectual ability and purported wisdom are not valued commodities in the animal kingdom. It's simple survival of the fittest. When the alpha cannot fight off a coup, he's aged out—and usually without ceremony.

Human beings have evolved to select leaders. In free societies, people follow leaders because they want to. We choose our leaders based largely on the qualities and characteristics we're going to explore in this book.

Leadership refers to the position or function of a leader. When I talk about leadership, I'm talking about the technical aspects that relate to function: skills, methodology, theory, and style.

When I talk about *the leader,* I'm talking specifically about the person and the essential human characteristics that transform an ordinary human being into an effective leader.

This is not a throwback to antiquated "great man" theories. I'll keep saying it—leaders are transformed, not born. Theories that center on characteristics alone are outdated. They're flawed because they assumed that the qualities that shaped a leader were innate traits bestowed by God or nature, or whatever universal force you might believe in. A leader was a leader by birthright, not by cultivation.

Today we understand that many characteristics of a leader can be developed through training. You can learn and cultivate these traits if you have good parents, effective teachers, and other influential people in your life.

However, I'm not a champion of the classic "trait theories" of leadership, either.

You can develop and cultivate the characteristics that can help you become a competent leader, but these traits do not guarantee that people are going to follow you. I will, though, argue the point that developing the characteristics shared by successful leaders is a damn good place to start!

Long after I realized from my own experience that a leader is transformed more than born or made, and several weeks after I wrote what I decided would be the opening line of this book, I found these words in the prologue of the classic text, *Leadership* by James MacGregor Burns:

> Assuming that leaders are neither "born" nor "made," we will look for patterns in the origins and socializing of persons that account for leadership.

I've got to tell you that when I read this passage, I felt as if those words were instantly familiar. I don't want to be overly sentimental—but Burns seemed to speak directly to my heart. I felt a connection to him like I felt with some of my masters whose lessons were new to me, but somehow instinctive and comfortable.

Burns was one of the first modern scholars to recognize the idea of *"transformational leadership."* Maybe that's the closest academic parallel to what I'm trying to share.

More from *Leadership:*

> ... the transforming leader looks for potential motives in followers, seeks to satisfy higher needs, and engages the full person of the follower. The result of transforming leadership is a relationship of mutual stimulation and elevation that converts followers into leaders and may convert leaders into moral agents.

Burns validates that leadership is an experience of the heart, not just an exercise for the mind.

He allows the word "transforming" to envelope the leader, the follower, and the relationship that defines them.

The relationship between leader and follower is, in itself, transformational. Again it's exactly the same as the relationship between the Sensei and the student; as you help others transform, you are transformed. You discover—or better yet, reveal the leader within you.

One of my masters used to say that the black belt isn't just a thing you strap on, it's something you carve out of yourself. It's like Michelangelo said:

"EVERY BLOCK OF STONE HAS A STATUE INSIDE IT AND IT IS THE TASK OF THE SCULPTOR TO DISCOVER IT."

The martial artist, like the sculptor, carves, shapes and polishes raw material into a useful form. The sculptor uses hammers and chisels to transform a block of stone into a work of art. The martial artist employs discipline and practice to transform a novice into a black belt.

A LEADER IS CARVED OUT OF EXPERIENCE

Experience is the hammer that transforms the knowledge, characteristics, and traits of leadership into something useful—the leader. You temper that experience through awareness into wisdom—one of the most distinctive qualities of an effective leader.

I'll talk much more about wisdom later. For now. I'm going to ask you to think about wisdom as the combination of knowledge and experience honed by awareness.

Wisdom is the cultivated sense of awareness you develop through self-examination, by constantly analyzing your experiences. If you're willing to look in the mirror, those experiences inform, inspire, and drive the process of your continual self-perfection and transformation.

Wisdom defines the transformational leader—someone with the ability to inspire others to dream, do and be more. I'm not talking about an elitist version of wisdom, the bearded hermit or the intelligentsia.

No. Wisdom is a readily available commodity, a quality anyone can develop in any number of useful areas—if you're willing to do the work.

Transformation defines effective leadership. In life and in business, if you are not changing, you are dying. One of the primary roles of a leader is to lead change and facilitate that process of transformation.

John P. Kotter, one of the most respected business minds in the world today, specifically defines leadership as your ability to deal with transformation and change:

"MANAGEMENT IS ABOUT COPING WITH COMPLEXITY. LEADERSHIP, BY CONTRAST, IS ABOUT COPING WITH CHANGE."

We can talk about "transformational leadership" in the

technical sense, as a leadership methodology, but that would be a tragic waste of the wisdom of Burns, Adams, Lao Tzu, and so many others. Understanding the leadership process, in itself, does not make anyone a leader.

Let's talk instead about the transformational leader. Let's focus on your capacity to lead others through the process of change.

The title of Sensei literally means: "one who went before."

As with any other talent, skill or ability, the best guide is usually the guy who walked the same path before you.

If a leader is someone who guides you through transformation, doesn't it make sense that the most effective leaders are those who have actually walked the walk?

WE'VE GOT A PROBLEM

Oh yes, we've got a problem today. We've got plenty of problems.

Here are some of the toughest ...

WE DON'T HAVE ENOUGH PEOPLE WILLING TO BECOME LEADERS

I don't blame them!

We treat celebrities like leaders. It's like some kind of high school popularity contest gone wild. We think somehow that because someone can act, shout or play a guitar, they know something more than the rest of us—this assumption can be extremely dangerous.

We treat authentic leaders like they're nuts—especially when they have the honesty and courage to hold up the mirror and show us that we've got hard work to do.

I don't think we have a lack of people with vision, but we certainly have become a culture where vision and innovation is approached with trepidation rather than embraced with enthusiasm or determination. We've become a people who like to play it safe, and that's reflected in the quality of our leadership.

We keep elevating people to leadership positions who promise us security and equanimity instead of those who are honest enough to talk about the risks and uncertainties that produce genuine opportunity and meaningful progress.

Someone with authority but without vision, without the courage for innovation, isn't a leader at all. At best that's a manager—at worst, a dictator.

When I'm talking about the genuine leader, I'm not talking about managers or elected officials or other people in classic positions of authority, God knows we've got plenty of those—too many! Too many without genuine leadership ability, that is.

I'm talking about the leaders we need at all levels.

We need to cultivate leaders with courage, compassion and wisdom at every level of our organizations and businesses. We need leadership on the front lines as well as the C-suite. We need leadership in our homes, our schools, and on our town councils as much as if not more than in the halls of Congress.

But, as I said, once we put a quality person in a position of leadership our next favorite pastime is knocking him back down again. That's something we need to change ...

... *now.*

WE'RE TOO DEPENDENT ON LEADERS

I don't believe we've entirely lost the spirit of rugged individualism—but it's sure as hell on life support!

For the first time in history, a nation was organized on the fundamental principle that the individual is superior to the state.

The United States was founded on the idea that you are endowed with "inalienable rights," and that it is the purpose of the state to protect those rights, not the purpose of the individual to serve king and country.

Has this experiment failed?

If we don't want to be ruled by kings, czars or dictators, then we've got to accept responsibility for ourselves. If we want to be citizens instead of subjects, we've got to govern and lead ourselves.

The same is true in business life where so many people stifle their own creativity waiting for ideas and orders from above. I don't have a problem with satisfied employees, but I have a huge disdain for people who complain about *"The Man"* and yet offer nothing in the way of ideas or solutions or worse.

Like so many in the Entitlement Generation, I used to bitch about *The Man* keeping me down too—until I realized one day that the only man responsible for my success is the same one looking at me every morning in that bathroom mirror I keep talking about.

We've got to stop depending on leaders, in the sense of

"others," to fulfill every need, grant every wish and solve every problem.

Our founders had the courage to reject the notion of a paternal nation to lead and govern themselves. We've got to reject the entitlement culture that looks to others, especially in the form of government, to provide for every basic need, grant every wish and solve every problem.

After all, didn't we once write a pretty impressive document that started with the words, *"We the People"*?

People who make the most effective leaders are usually people who don't want and don't need overbearing, paternalistic or authoritarian leadership.

These days we seldom rally around a leader with the courage to be honest when times are tough or the leader who calls on our ingenuity and grit when we're faced with the most difficult challenges or choices. Instead, we flock to the leader that promises easy solutions or the charismatic leader who satisfies some misplaced and distorted yearning for paternal guidance and security.

It's time to stop being a society of children and start building a culture of leadership again.

LEADERS ARE WASTING TOO MUCH TIME DEFENDING THEIR TURF

People in authority positions invest entirely too much time and energy defending their ground and protecting their position. This is the natural defense mechanism of the incompetent leader.

When we don't choose leaders with good character, we end up with people in positions of authority who will inevitably defend their reputations and territory out of insecurity, incompetence or just plain jealousy.

Turf battles are destructive to the group, the organization and the community. A genuine leader does not have to protect turf.

Power expands through sharing, and that's what happens in an organization with a strong leadership culture.

In this culture people don't waste valuable time and resources defending turf. Instead, they invest their energy in developing more leaders.

WE TOO OFTEN CONFUSE AUTHORITY AND LEADERSHIP

The best leaders in any group are quite often standing next to you, or even below you—rather than above you. This is why it's important to invest in leadership at all levels, independent of a person's position of authority.

Leadership is a quality of the person expressed by a willingness to act first, to ask before being asked, to share experience and wisdom without conditions.

Authority is the right or privilege granted a particular individual to exercise command and control.

The problem is that authority can, and often does, exist independently of authentic leadership.

The flip side is that effective leadership can, and should, exist regardless of one's position of authority, and that's a good thing. We'll dig deeper into this in a later chapter.

Some of your best leaders have absolutely no interest in authority. They're not motivated by title or position. Their motivation is doing their best, helping others do their best, and knowing that their role is valued.

We need more of those leaders at all levels.

TOO MANY PEOPLE IN LEADERSHIP POSITIONS STOP DEVELOPING AS LEADERS

Some have never really learned how to be leaders in the first place, or they've just become complacent. They assume their certificates, rank and titles somehow grant them leadership credentials—just as the scarecrow thought a diploma gave him brains.

The most effective and genuine leaders never stop learning, growing and developing.

THE MOST DANGEROUS PROBLEM

The most dangerous problem in leadership today is the lingering disconnect between organizational leadership and personal or interpersonal leadership.

We've got to restore humanity to leadership. After all,

leadership is a uniquely human experience.

I'm not going to talk a lot about the technical or academic aspects of leadership—

I'm here to talk about the leader.

I have earned a few degrees—of Black Belt, but I've never earned a formal degree in leadership studies or management.

I learned about leadership by becoming a leader.

My job is to help you identify, understand and cultivate the fundamental human characteristics that will help you become a more effective leader. My hope is that you embrace the role of the Sensei by teaching and mentoring others to become effective leaders, at all levels, independent of their authority and independent of their ambitions.

This book is about the *human* experience of the leader.

We've got to take care not to lose the human aspects of leadership to process.

YOU DON'T LEAD PROCESS— YOU LEAD PEOPLE

Genuine leadership is expressed as an ability to inspire and direct the collective efforts of *people.*

We've built business and political systems and processes that connect us around the world. We've constructed systems, infrastructures and machinery that give us almost unimaginable access to power and productivity. At the same time, we've unintentionally created a widening gap between the leaders and the people who make these systems work.

This gap is expensive — very expensive.

Over 70% of our workforce worldwide is disengaged. The primary causes all relate to leadership, or more accurately, distrust or lack of it. The losses directly related to disengagement are staggering, measured in billions nationally, trillions globally.

A very interesting study by the HR firm Adecco, as reported in *Fast Company,* highlights a horrifying disconnect between management and employees. They took a hard look at what employees want from leadership, what they're actually getting, and even more revealing—what the bosses thought they were delivering.

> Only 15% of bosses described their own management style as commanding. About 23% of employees, on the other hand, reported their boss's style to be commanding, and just 11% said being commanding was the desired style. "Bosses may not recognize how bossy they actually are," the report says.

The story continues …

> Similarly, bosses believe they are visionary leaders and good coaches; their employees disagree. "Nearly one in three bosses may think they are using a coaching style, but only one in five employees agrees," concludes Adecco. Only 17% of bosses are self-styled visionaries, whereas close to 23% of employees view this as the preferred leadership style.

They also reported that 1 in 3 people considered themselves smarter than the boss, at the same time—*fewer people want to be the boss!*

With young people, it's even worse. Nearly half of them think they're smarter than the boss, yet only 30% have defined leadership ambitions.

If this generational gap isn't addressed, and soon, most of the people you lead in the future will think they can do your job better than you can—but they won't be willing to step up and do anything about it! You can imagine the motivation and engagement problems associated with that dynamic.

As bad as things are in business leadership, it's even worse in politics ...

ABC News/Washington Post polling indicates that just 27% plan to vote for an incumbent. As of this writing in 2014, only 37% trust the President to make the right decision, and Congress is in the tank with just a 16% approval rating.

At least two generations have been so disenchanted and feel so powerless that we now have a severe leadership shortage in government, business and the community. People are simply not willing to serve in such futile and thankless leadership positions.

A study by Richard L. Fox of Loyola Marymount University and Jennifer L. Lawless of American University measured interest in holding political office. They found that only 3% of people belonging to groups that typically produce candidates reported that they would "definitely" run for office.

It's worth mentioning that their report was intended to measure whether political ambition increases or wanes over time.

Want to guess what they found?

I'll leave it to you to read the reports. I don't want to turn this book into an academic thesis or a commentary on other people's research. All that information is readily available, and it's not hard to find.

My focus is on how to develop effective leaders, the kind of leaders we want and need in business, in politics, and in our local communities.

My mission is to cultivate the type of leader who understands that leadership is an essential human responsibility.

My job is to help you develop as a leader, and to help you develop leaders at all levels who understand that each of us must accept the responsibility of leadership, even if we don't fit the conventional model of the "leader."

Today, sadly enough, popularity, charisma and empty promises too often trump intelligence, substance and sincerity when it comes to choosing our leaders. Rather than being recognized as a hero, an authentic leader today is as likely to become the target of the torch and pitchfork brigade.

WHY WOULD ANYONE STILL WANT TO ACCEPT THE BURDEN OF LEADERSHIP?

I'm not sure that I have a good answer to that question!

For me, it's enough to know that despite this challenging

environment, or maybe because of it, there are still people willing to step up and become leaders.

If I haven't discouraged you yet, chances are you're one of those people ...

... and we need you!

主
領

STUDENT TO
TEACHER

*The first step in any transformation is recognizing
the need for a change.*

It doesn't matter whether you're trying to overcome an addiction or other personal setback or you're trying to lead a
large company through a significant period of change or innovation. Along the way you encounter people who can help
or guide you through the process of transformation.

Sometimes we call these people mentors, sometimes we
give them C-level titles—we call others consultants, mentors
or coaches.

No matter what we call these people, they have one fundamental role …

… teacher.

In my life, many of my teachers were "Sensei."

Sensei is a Japanese term—most people these days would translate the word as "teacher." That works.

The Sensei is a teacher, coach and mentor. But most of all, the genuine Sensei is a leader.

Sensei means "one who went before." The assumption is that someone recognized as a Sensei has walked the walk and can lead you down the same path.

When I started my first dojo, I was very grateful for the lessons I learned from several of the teachers, Sensei, that I'd encountered along the way. Some of them were still actively in my life, but others had long since been left behind for one reason or another.

Many were martial artists; others were teachers from other adventures.

I had teachers from business, teachers from the world of marketing and sales, teachers and supervisors from the various jobs that I've held—and I've had my share of jobs!

Others were simply remarkable people I'd met along the way.

I always tell new instructors and dojo operators that in the role of Sensei they'll use every experience they've ever had in their lives, and they'd better brace themselves for plenty more. The same is true for leaders, no matter what business or occupation you might pursue.

In these first few years of running my own dojo, I came to appreciate the principle that a good teacher must first be a good student; a good leader must first be a good follower.

Great leaders continue to be good followers!

The difference between a leader and a follower, at any given time, is just a matter of which role you're playing. It's a lot like dancing; you've got to learn when to lead—and when to follow.

Effective leaders understand leading and following as a dynamic interplay of roles ...

... not a static position.

MY FIRST SENSEI

I want to go back to those first few steps up—and then back down those dojo stairs.

Sometimes you cross paths with someone for the briefest of moments, yet that person makes a profound and lasting impression. I've been blessed with several of these encounters.

My very brief time with my first Sensei was one of those.

Dick Roy embodied the principles he shared with us. I don't know if he was the greatest martial artist around, as far as I knew he was. More important to me was his sincerity, humanness and his dedication to his craft and his students. I didn't get involved in martial arts to become a fighter, I did it to find myself.

One evening Dick Sensei announce that he was going to spar with all the students. I have to say, I almost shit myself!

At this time, I was just about two years from being a malnourished drug addict. I'd been an athlete in my younger days—I'd even played semi-pro soccer before I started smoking pot. Having been an athlete only made it worse! I could feel how far I'd fallen every time I took a fall.

I was outmatched sparring with the senior students. I was

enthusiastic enough and was no longer flinching every time someone blinked, but my skills were still very raw.

If these guys were taking it to me, what was going to happen when I squared off against Sensei?

I had not yet developed what I now call the *"Christmas Spirit in Fighting."* That means when it comes to pain, it's much better to give than to receive! At this point, I was the joyful recipient of most of the blows in most of my matches.

The thought of facing off against Dick Sensei was, to put a shine on it, intimidating. The only thing that kept me from chickening out was watching some of my buddies survive the first few rounds.

Then it was my turn ...

Sensei was the Tasmanian devil.

I don't remember a damn thing, and I don't really think I saw even one of the punches and kicks he landed at will.

The only punch I do remember is the last one.

Sensei caught me with a straight jab—I saw a flash of light and my legs turned to rubber. I knew afterwards that he pulled the punch in an attempt to keep me safe—you don't sign up a lot of new students by knocking them out, but I ran straight into it.

I don't know how I stayed on my feet, but I finished the round.

The only reason I didn't feel completely emasculated was that I hadn't done any worse than anyone else at my level that night. Still, I was plenty humbled and ready for Sensei's critique—which I was sure would sting even worse than his punches.

Dick Sensei was not that type of teacher.

Before I knew what was happening, Sensei grabbed me in a big bear hug and slapped me in the head.

I don't remember exactly what he said, it was something like, *"I'm proud of you! You take a great shot—you're a tough guy!"*

After we all finished our turn, Sensei gathered us around to stretch and cool down. He started to talk, slowly, quietly:

"I'm proud of every one of you. It takes guts to stay in there when you you're up against a better fighter.

"Every one of you stood your ground. *That's what it's all about."*

An effective leader is one who has the ability to develop willing followers—and nothing helps develop willing followers more than the sincere and compassionate encouragement of a respected teacher.

THE TRANSFORMATION FROM STUDENT TO TEACHER

Around 1994 I founded my own martial arts organization, Northern Chi Martial Arts Centers.

Like the leader of any new organization, I wanted to create a logo, a crest, to symbolize my vision for the organization and the principles that it would represent and embody. I poured over hundreds of various symbols and graphics— some traditional, some contemporary, in search of some way to express my core philosophies visually.

On the crest I placed three symbolic figures of a person in a martial arts on-guard posture. These three figures represent the relationships necessary for the meaningful personal transformation from beginner to Black Belt ...

... from follower to leader.

1. TEACHER GUIDES THE STUDENT

You can easily substitute the words leader and follower for teacher and student.

The new student or follower depends on the teacher or leader for instruction, guidance, correction, and encouragement. At this point, the student knows little or nothing about the journey ahead of him. Right now the teacher is mostly giving, the student receiving.

As one of my most influential teachers, Dr. Yang, Jwing-Ming would say, "It is the teacher's responsibility to teach. It is the students responsibility to learn."

That's a great job description for each role during these first steps.

2. STUDENT TO STUDENT

The next relationship is *"student to student."* This is when peer to peer leadership becomes an important part of the process.

You find out very early in your martial arts training that most learning comes through experience. The Sensei guides you, but you're going to experience most of your growth and development by doing—by training with your peers.

This relationship is dynamic and fluid.

As you train and develop, you may take the lead at times.

At other times you follow and submit yourself to the leadership and guidance of your peers.

Fighting, and learning how to fight, is a lot like dancing!

3. STUDENT BECOMES THE TEACHER

Finally, you become the Sensei. The relationship is transformational at this point as the student becomes the teacher.

You ARE the one who went before.

You've walked a few miles by now. You've become the leader. It's now your responsibility to guide the next generation of new students through their first steps.

What happens when you reach that final stage?

The trip starts all over again. Better yet, you start a new, even more challenging adventure.

This process is cyclical, not linear, and when you fully embrace this process, the cycle is not fixed, but ever-expanding.

The Sensei leader seeks out new adventures, new challenges. There are always new talents, skills and abilities to develop, new levels of proficiency and new ways to apply our talents, experience and hopefully by now, our wisdom.

Embrace this process, and you'll become much more effective as a leader—a Master, in the truest sense of the word.

主
領

HARD SKILLS VS. SOFT SKILLS

Yes, strength and hardness accompany death, softness and weakness accompany life.

And so: With a battle axe too hardened you cannot win. When a tree becomes hard, then comes the axe.

~Lao Tzu

Martial arts are generally divided into two major categories: hard styles and soft styles.

Hard styles emphasize explosive expression of power. Think of most karate styles, *Tae Kwon Do,* and kickboxing.

The soft styles like *Tai Chi* and *Aikido* emphasize connectivity and efficiency. Techniques favor deflection over stopping power, leverage over brute strength.

You can see the same divide in business and professional development.

"Hard" skills refer to technical and domain training, whereas *"soft"* skills include personal development areas—character development, communication and listening skills, empathy, mentoring, and of course, leadership training.

In many organizations, technical management training would be classified as a *"hard"* skill, while leadership theory and personal development might be considered *"soft."*

WHICH IS MORE EFFECTIVE— MORE POWERFUL?

My early experiences in martial arts focused entirely system called *Kenpo Karate.* About a year after I got my Black Belt, our organization started to integrate Tai Chi, what seemed to me to be a radically different style and approach.

I was obsessed with this new perspective. From the start, I was much more interested in the philosophy of the arts than the physicality. At this point, I was desperate for some kind of philosophical and spiritual fulfillment in my life, and Tai Chi seemed to fill the gap.

I immediately faced a huge obstacle. Like many students exposed to a new way of doing things, the new way challenged and often seemed to contradict everything I had learned up to that point. I was excited, but confused.

I decided to ask my Kenpo Master outright if our style was considered "hard" or "soft." His response was direct and certain: "Hard." End of discussion.

A lot of leaders express that same macho attitude when they express a bias for hard skills development over soft in the workplace.

At any rate, my Master saw Tai Chi more or less as an interesting distraction—and a way to generate a new revenue stream, but he considered himself a hard-core "hard" stylist.

I could certainly still appreciate the explosive power of Kenpo, but I was also experiencing a new level of power through the soft principles of deflection, leverage, and borrowing my opponent's force. I also started to recognize that while the ethnocentric stance was to embrace Kenpo as a hard, probably more "macho" style, if you will, it seemed to me that the two styles had a lot more similarities than differences—if you knew how to look for them.

A typical soft style technique you might learn in Tai Chi or Aikido is the principle of *borrowing*, or multiplying power by using the power of the attacker against him. You'll learn more about that when we talk about tactics later—but here's a quick example:

A 200 pound man running at you with head full of hate

can generate an impact force of 1600 pounds or more. If you employ strict hard style technique, you might choose to stop that force by direct resistance. Head to head, you need 1600 pounds of force or more to stop your attacker in his tracks, and a lot more if you want to knock him on his back.

What if instead of meeting your attacker's force head on, you step to the side and deflect his force?

Even better—time his attack and as he makes his run, intercept him from an angle, and help him to the ground with the combined power of his attack plus the added energy of your response.

Transfer this idea to a leadership scenario ...

Say that you're charged with introducing a new innovation or a change in policy, but you immediately face resistance to that change.

Is it better to meet resistance head on? Or is it usually more effective to understand the reasoning behind the resistance and develop a consensus—a buy in?

How effective is total authoritarianism?

Isn't it more effective to solicit the support of everyone involved to access the full potential of their skills, talents and enthusiasm to implement the change?

Both hard and soft have their appropriate applications. The trick is to know which tactic to use in which situation.

Whether you're using a hard or soft technique, you're

looking for exactly the same thing …

… power.

And leadership is all about power—if you understand the true meaning of power:

POWER IS YOUR ABILITY OR CAPACITY TO ACT OR PERFORM EFFECTIVELY.

That's it.

Leadership is an articulate expression of power—your ability to act effectively to get something done—hopefully something meaningful.

Become powerful and you will be more effective. Help others become powerful, and you're a leader.

But I still haven't given you a direct answer to the question that started this chapter.

Which is more powerful? Which is more effective? Hard or soft?

A well rounded fighter, or leader, is skilled in hard and soft styles and can use either or a combination of both to best advantage in a given situation.

But, after years of study and practice—I have to give the edge to the soft styles.

I said earlier that the hard styles are generally additive. That is, to gain more power in a hard style technique you add something—more range of movement, more intensity, more strength, or more speed.

The soft styles are subtractive. You increase power by decreasing resistance and tension. You increase power through efficiency and leverage—not by increasing input energy.

Apply this thinking to business and leadership philosophy. Technical or hard skills are important and have their application, but you increase the effectiveness and efficiency of those techniques exponentially when you have the right mindset, the qualities and characteristics that make you more effective as a leader—the so called soft skills.

NO HARD LEADERSHIP OR MANAGEMENT
TECHNIQUE OR PROCESS WILL WORK
EFFECTIVELY UNLESS THE LEADER
POSSESSES THE SOFT SKILLS NECESSARY
TO ATTRACT WILLING FOLLOWERS,
INSPIRE THEM, AND ENGENDER THEIR
SUPPORT AND LOYALTY.

In the next two sections, we're going to talk about the qualities of an effective leader and the techniques of leadership.

Look at the qualities of the leader as the "soft" aspects, and the strategies, techniques, and tactics of leadership as the "hard."

The qualities of the leader are those human characteristics and traits that define your capacity to be a leader.

Qualities must be *identified, cultivated, developed,* and then *expressed.*

Techniques are *learned, assimilated,* and *applied.*

Of the two, the qualities of the leader are more important. As you develop the qualities that will make you a capable leader, you increase your capacity to lead effectively using any of the strategies, tactics, and techniques you can master. Without those qualities, the strategies and tactics we're going to share can be just as easily exploited by the tyrant.

General Norman Schwartzkopf said:

"LEADERSHIP IS A POTENT COMBINATION OF STRATEGY AND CHARACTER. BUT IF YOU MUST BE WITHOUT ONE—

"BE WITHOUT THE STRATEGY."

PART TWO
THE ESSENTIAL CHARACTERISTICS OF THE SENSEI LEADER

主
領

THE ESSENTIAL CHARACTERISTICS

"WISDOM, COMPASSION, AND COURAGE
ARE THE THREE UNIVERSALLY
RECOGNIZED MORAL QUALITIES
OF MEN."

~ CONFUCIUS

I had never heard this quote when I started looking for the most essential qualities of an effective leader. I arrived at these three qualities by asking kids what they were looking for in a leader.

That's right—kids.

For about 3 years I did an exercise with Junior Instructor trainees in my martial arts program. I asked them to come up with three words to describe a leader, someone they would follow willingly.

They came up with the same three words Confucius preached so long ago.

I do the same exercise in my corporate and conference workshops. No matter what age, what occupation or what demographic category, most people identify the same qualities these kids did year after year:

COURAGE

COMPASSION

WISDOM

You could certainly add to the list, but limiting the list forces us to identify the most essential qualities—those qualities without which you simply cannot consider yourself an authentic or effective leader. Every suggestion I've ever heard fits into one of these three buckets.

It's simple.

Commit yourself to continual development and cultivation in these three areas, and you will become a more effective and capable leader. Commit yourself to helping others develop these characteristics, and your power and effectiveness as a leader expands exponentially.

BE A LEADER, NOT A DICTATOR

There is a huge difference between a leader and a dictator.

A leader is someone who has the ability to attract willing followers—emphasis on willing.

A dictator is someone who commands through fear, force, deception or coercion.

Be careful—some dictators are extremely charismatic.

Many dictators are skilled at making themselves attractive to the masses. Some are masters of exploiting populist sentiment. They look, walk and talk like leaders, but when they're crossed, their real aim is to show you who's boss.

The dictator inevitably resorts to brute force and intimidation to get his way. Out of necessity if not by design, control becomes his essential guiding principle.

Control is not a priority for the true leader. In fact, some degree of comfort with uncertainty is a powerful quality of effective leaders and a good indicator of a future leader's potential.

A leader must be strong, decisive, and sometimes even authoritative, but in the long run the genuine leader is someone who earns sincere trust and loyalty. People follow a leader of their own free will.

Speaking from personal experience ranging from Marine Corps captain to Presidential cabinet secretary, John W. Gardner wrote:

"LEADERS CANNOT MAINTAIN AUTHORITY ... UNLESS FOLLOWERS ARE PREPARED TO BELIEVE IN THAT AUTHORITY."

The dictator believes that his authority is granted by some power other than the belief and consent of followers and that his subjects serve him. The dictator places self-interest, personal safety and selfish expediency above the care of others.

The authentic leader serves the people.

The leader places the needs and ambitions of others in equal, if not superior position to his own.

The leader understands that his authority is a product of trust. His position is secured by consent of the people under his responsibility.

The authority of the leader is earned ...

... through Courage, Compassion, and Wisdom.

COURAGE

Courage is not the absence of fear. The absence of fear is stupidity.

General George S. Patton, my favorite leader-warrior, said:

> If we take the generally accepted definition of bravery as a quality which knows no fear, I have never seen a brave man. All men are frightened. The more intelligent they are, the more they are frightened.

Everyone, especially rational people, experience fear. It's natural. Fear is part of our survival mechanism. Fear is what separates the brave from the foolish.

Without fear, there is no courage.

Any idiot can charge into trouble ignorant of danger. Your courage is defined by your awareness of the risk involved.

COURAGE IS YOUR ABILITY TO FACE YOUR FEAR AND DO WHAT NEEDS TO BE DONE IN SPITE OF IT.

Of all the qualities of an effective leader, courage is the most iconic, and people expect you to have it.

Usually, people will forgive your mistakes and transgressions, sometimes to a surprising degree. They'll overlook shortcomings, lack of knowledge, incompetence and even deception …

… but they'll never follow a coward.

Always remember—*courage is not the absence of fear.*

People expect you to be afraid at times, but they always expect to keep moving—even if you're scared. They expect you to carry the flag when they're afraid and sometimes when you're afraid—they expect you to act as if you're not!

I won't sugar-coat it. At times, the ability to look and speak bravely when you're scared is a tremendously useful talent for a leader. However, what you do in the face of fear is infinitely more important than what you say, what game face you put on, or how hard you thump your chest.

THIS IS WHAT COURAGE LOOKS LIKE

One of the most impressive acts of courage I've witnessed, and I've seen my share, was the action of a 12 year-old girl in my martial arts program.

Jennifer and all of her five brothers and sisters, with the exception of a newborn infant, were students in my program. On this particular afternoon, her two younger brothers were scheduled for private lessons. About the time their lessons were supposed to start, Jennifer walked in the door to tell me that her mother was not feeling well and asked if they could reschedule the lessons.

I said sure—and that I hoped her Mom would feel better soon.

Jennifer said thank you—but she looked very upset and nervous.

She was a shy girl, but she was always a ray of sunshine. I'd never seen her this way. I asked what was wrong with her mother.

She said she wasn't sure.

Mom had been driving them to the center and just started acting strange. She had started weaving on the road and was having a very hard time focusing on her driving. She had also started talking funny. Jennifer knew something was wrong, but wasn't sure what it could be. At any rate, since they were almost to the dojo, they had just decided to stop in and then they were heading home.

I asked Jen where her Mom was right now. She told me her mother was waiting in the car. Jen was worried because it seemed like Mom couldn't stay awake.

I knew for a fact that Jennifer's mother did not drink—even if she did, I could not imagine her endangering her children. She is the mother that every other mother on this earth should pattern herself after.

I'd been an Emergency Medical Technician in one of my

past lives. Given her symptoms, I suspected Jen's Mom might be having a stroke. I went out to the car to see what I could make of the situation.

Mom recognized me, but was making no sense. It was obvious that she was in distress, and everything I could see confirmed my suspicions—I now knew this was a stroke.

I took Mom into the building and called for an ambulance. Meanwhile, I asked Jen if she could help with the baby and the other kids. At this point, she knew the situation was serious and she was doing her best to fight back tears.

I've seen adults go to pieces in similar situations. Jen rallied, got the baby from the car seat and got her brothers and sisters situated in the lobby.

In the middle of all of this, I asked Jen if she could call her Dad. Unfortunately, Dad was out of town on business. Jen suggested we call her grandmother.

As we waited for grandma and the ambulance to arrive, Jen was the embodiment of courage. She remained calm and did her best to comfort her brothers and sisters, who were all visibly shaken by the scenario.

That kid never shed a tear until after the ambulance left and her grandmother arrived to pick up the family.

Jen's mother eventually made a remarkable recovery and in fact, part of her recovery included Natural Motion Martial Arts, a remarkable program for people with brain injuries founded by Shawn Withers, one of our Black Belt graduates and author of *Broken Wing*, the remarkable story of his own recovery from a devastating stroke.

Some time after the incident I had a chance to talk with Jennifer and hear her feelings on the adventure. That conversation revealed how terrified she had been that day—and how aware she was that something very serious and dangerous was happening.

As scared as she was, she managed her fear and did what needed to be done.

In my opinion, she acted more courageously than most people—of any age.

3 TYPES OF COURAGE

There are three types of courage: *heroic, artistic* and *moral*. It's important for a leader to understand and practice each one.

HEROIC COURAGE

This one is obvious. Heroic courage is what you witness when a warrior charges into battle or a firefighter runs into a burning building.

ARTISTIC COURAGE

Artistic courage is the courage to expose your ideas to public scrutiny. It's the courage to explore and develop your talents, skills and abilities.

In business, it's the courage to transform your ideas into products and services and test those ideas in the market. It's the courage you need to lead change and innovation.

MORAL COURAGE

Moral courage is the courage to do the right thing—even when it's not expedient, comfortable or popular.

As a leader today, your moral courage will be challenged nearly every single day. Too many leaders fail to answer this challenge. If we have any hope of restoring a culture of leadership, we've got to reverse this trend.

Do the right thing.

You might be called to act with courage at any time, but how can you guarantee you'll act courageously when that call comes?

Unfortunately, you can't. When it comes to courage, you'll only know with absolute certainty how you'll act when the time comes.

You can, however, increase the odds that you'll act courageously. Courage is the manifestation of genuine confidence.

Genuine confidence is the product of training ...

TRAIN TO BE COURAGEOUS

"IT SEEMS TO ME I DID NO MORE THAN
SHOULD HAVE BEEN EXPECTED OF ME,
AND WHAT IT WAS MY DUTY TO DO
UNDER THE SUDDEN AND GREAT
RESPONSIBILITIES WHICH FELL
UPON ME THERE."

~JOSHUA L. CHAMBERLAIN

Can you really train and prepare yourself to act courageously when the time comes?

I've already made the argument that even with the best training, you can't anticipate every possible variable and you can't guarantee any particular outcome …

… but you can sure as hell improve your odds!

The more focused, sincere and comprehensive your training, the more likely you are to perform under pressure. You can't control all the conditions you might face, but you can control how well prepared you are to respond to whatever those conditions and circumstances might be.

As I said, heroic courage is probably the most obvious type of courage—but it's also the rarest kind. It's not that people don't want to act heroically, it's just that most people will seldom if ever get the opportunity.

If you're a soldier, a firefighter, a cop or first responder, you might face daily opportunities to test your capacity for heroic courage. For the rest of us it's almost impossible to practice heroic courage simply because—fortunately, the opportunity just doesn't come along very often.

Still, you are capable of acting heroically, when and if you're ever called to be the hero, if you train properly. The key is practice.

This is exactly why martial artists practice self-defense scenarios ...

Most of us will never be the victim of a violent attack, again—fortunately!

Since we don't have the opportunity to test our skills regularly against a real attacker, we design scenarios so we can practice and condition our response.

We try to anticipate as many variables as possible—angles of attack, weapons, multiple attackers. We practice as many combinations of these variables as possible and design exercises that give us the opportunity to respond to unanticipated changes on the fly.

Of course there are other factors that affect how you'll perform in the face of real danger including the level of threat, your physical condition at the time, the possible risk to others in the area, and the element of surprise.

You have no control over most of these factors ...

... but you always have full control over your training and preparation.

What conditions can you anticipate facing in your personal and professional life?

What techniques are readily available for you to learn and practice?

How can you train yourself to respond to changing conditions and surprises?

Captain Chesley "Sully" Sullenberger is the hero who safely piloted US Airways flight 1549 into the Hudson River after a bird strike disabled his plane in January, 2009. His courage helped him save everyone aboard.

Where did his courage come from? How did he stay so calm in such a dangerous situation?

Training.

The amazing story of Sullivan piloting the plane and landing in the East River is a classic example of someone who was prepared to act courageously when the time came.

Even though he had not practiced the exact scenario he encountered over the Hudson, his training gave him an arsenal of possible reactions and the capability to adapt his skills to a rapidly changing situation.

He logged thousands of hours in all types of aircraft and like all pilots, he continually analyzed and improved his performance. He spent hours in simulators practicing for possible emergencies similar to the one he faced that day.

His training gave him the confidence to act calmly and rationally under pressure. He was prepared to respond to unanticipated conditions and circumstances. He was confident in his ability to perform to his best to the end—no matter what the outcome.

His lifetime commitment to training prepared Captain Sullivan to act with courage when faced with the worst scenario imaginable.

You can prepare yourself to be a hero, too.

Your capacity to act with courage increases in direct proportion to your dedication to preparation, training and practice.

PREPARE OTHERS TO ACT COURAGEOUSLY—TRAIN THEM TOO!

Courage is a potential, a capacity.

Your potential to act courageously increases with genuine confidence. You grow that confidence through preparation, training and discipline.

You develop confidence by exposing yourself to ever greater challenges and by doing what it takes to meet those challenges.

Part of your role as a leader is to provide and even design opportunities for others to test their talents, skills and abilities and develop their confidence and courage.

That's the reason for all our pretty colored belts in martial arts. Each belt represents a new level of learning, an advancement in skill and understanding and an opportunity to meet ever more demanding tests and challenges at each rank.

Each rank is a small step on the longer journey. A student might not be able to see the end of the journey, but he can see the next objective.

Your job is to design a progressive series of challenges that

70

provide the opportunity for growth in attainable steps. Each step should build confidence while still providing enough of a challenge so that it requires a person's best efforts to achieve the next level.

Design the test, then give people the space to perform. In his book, *Patton on Leadership,* Alan Axelrod added this commentary:

> Train and prepare the members of your organization, then get out of their way as much as possible. Don't fail to monitor progress, but don't breathe down anyone's neck either.

Or do it as the General himself did:

"ONCE, IN SICILY, I TOLD A GENERAL, WHO WAS SOMEWHAT RELUCTANT TO ATTACK, THAT I HAD PERFECT CONFIDENCE IN HIM, AND THAT, TO SHOW IT, I WAS GOING HOME."

That's how you build confidence—and that's how you develop courage.

WILL YOU HAVE THE COURAGE TO DO THE RIGHT THING?

> "THE SUPERIOR MAN THINKS ALWAYS OF VIRTUE—THE COMMON MAN THINKS OF COMFORT."
>
> ~CONFUCIUS

Moral courage is your willingness to do what is right—even when it's not comfortable, convenient, expedient or profitable.

Research consistently shows that trust is one of the most desired traits in a leader.

If you want people to follow you willingly, they've got to be able to trust you. You build trust by doing the right thing.

I'm sure you'd like to think you'd do the right thing under any circumstances, but doing the right thing can cost you money, your reputation, your business or even your safety or your life.

What are you really willing to do when you're faced with

these choices?

Moral courage can be heroic, but in most cases, a moral dilemma does not involve a risk to life or limb. The most difficult moral challenges often deal with our response to authority.

You've got to understand this problem from both sides— from the perspective of the follower as well as the leader:

Are you willing to carry out orders you know are just plain wrong?

Are you sure in what direction your moral compass is pointing?

Do your followers see you as a moral and ethical leader?

Would you ever ask someone to do something they consider wrong?

Never underestimate your power to influence the actions of devoted followers.

The infamous and controversial "Milgram Experiment" sought to test the limits of moral courage.

From *SimplyPsychology.com* ...

> Stanley Milgram, a psychologist at Yale University, conducted an experiment focusing on the conflict between obedience to authority and personal conscience.

He examined justifications for acts of genocide offered by those accused at the World War II, Nuremberg War Criminal trials. Their defense often was based on "obedience" - that they were just following orders from their superiors.

There is a ton of readily available information and commentary on Milgram, so I won't bore you with the details.

For those who may not be familiar with his experiments, he tested subjects to see if they would administer what they thought were dangerous, maybe even lethal levels of electric shocks under orders from an authority figure.

You'd probably like to think that you would never administer a shock to another person—even under orders—not a shock that would cause pain or discomfort—and certainly not with enough intensity to cause someone's death.

If so, you'd be the exception, not the rule.

Fully 65% of the participants in this experiment were willing to jolt another human being with full voltage—*even though they knew they were possibly doing great harm—maybe even causing the death of another human being.*

Later attempts to replicate Milgram's results showed flaws in some aspects of his methodology, especially the fact that he didn't counsel his subjects following the experiment.

Many of them were severely traumatized by the experience!

Still, this infamous experiment serves as a stunning example of what can happen if we lack the moral courage to resist immoral authority, even when—or *especially* when we know we're doing wrong.

The most important aspect of this experiment involves something Milgram called the *"agentic state."*

The agentic state makes you more likely to turn up the juice on your fellow man when you believe that you're acting under orders from someone you consider to be a legitimate authority figure.

As I said, a leader has to understand and appreciate this phenomenon from both the perspective of the leader and the follower.

We can't dismiss the responsibility of the follower in this relationship. We train our military personnel to refuse to carry out immoral orders—though that line is often blurred under the real stress of combat.

As a leader, however, you must understand that some people will tend to follow your instructions simply because they trust you or respect your authority. Your position of superiority might give, in their minds, a moral "hall pass" to do things they otherwise might never consider.

Sadly, there is nothing you can do that *absolutely* assures that you—or your followers—will act courageously and do the right thing when faced with a serious moral dilemma. People do strange things under pressure.

You can, however, greatly increase the probability that you'll act courageously by training your ethical mind.

Ask yourself ...

Would you refuse orders, even if doing so risked your job or career? Where would you draw the line?

Would you speak out if you saw someone else being abused or mistreated at work? What if the instigator is your boss?

Would you ever lie to protect yourself, your job or your reputation? If so, under what conditions?

Would you ever cheat or lie if a large amount of money were on the line? How much would it take to get you to cross the line?

Don't wait until you're actually face to face with situations that test your moral courage. Too many leaders have waited until they faced real moral dilemmas to decide what to do—many of them failed the test.

Imagine possible situations and conditions you might face in the future. Decide what you would do—then practice and reinforce that thinking to give you the best possible chance to act with true moral courage when you most need to.

Just as martial artists practice their responses to potential physical attacks, practice your responses to possible threats to your moral integrity.

Create opportunities to openly discuss difficult moral and ethical issues. Design appropriate protocols.

Share this process with others, especially with children—and employees.

Speaking of kids, they usually have an innate desire to do the right thing—until we teach them how to do wrong!

Here's an interesting study in moral courage from one of our recent Junior Black Belt tests …

Throughout the test the instructors hand one of the candidates a page with a difficult ethical problem. Their job is work with the other candidates and come up with some sort of solution in about 30 seconds.

This is one of the questions we use:

> Your friends are teasing a kid at school. This kid is kind of weird and nobody, including you, particularly likes him.

> Your friends are egging you on to join in the fun. You know that if you don't, your friends are going to start in on you.

What do you do?

I expected part, but not all, of the solution they came up with.

At first they said they'd try to offer friendship to the kid the others targeted. That was in keeping with what we taught and consistent with the character of our young leaders.

I wanted to test them a little harder ...

"It isn't easy making friends sometimes, is it?" I asked. "What are you going to do if your other friends turn their backs on you?"

One particular candidate was a kid who really had to work to fit in. I knew from past stories that he could easily have been the kid we described in our scenario. He spoke up:

"If they want to treat someone like that. They're no friends to me."

That is leadership at it's most fundamental and most important level.

Lately, I've been seriously concerned that authentic leadership is a dying art. These kids are helping to restore my faith.

The scenario we gave these kids is strikingly similar to documented incidents of workplace bullying and incivility.

How would you respond given a similar situation in the workplace?

Authentic leadership is not complicated. It's not a product of academic knowledge, research or analysis.

Leadership is paying attention to the fundamental needs, desires and ambitions of the people who trust you to serve. It's being attuned on a deeply personal level with the humanity of the people you serve.

It's doing what is right for them even when it's not easy, convenient or expedient.

These kids will face problems much more difficult than a hypothetical scenario in a safe and controlled testing environment—but this is where it starts.

I'm very confident this group of remarkable young people

will grow to be excellent Black Belts and, more important, genuine leaders.

If they can do it, so can we.

ARTISTIC COURAGE: THE COURAGE TO CREATE

Writing for *Forbes.com*, Bruce Rogers highlighted an address by Kevin Spacey at the *SapientNitro Idea Exchange* in New York City.

Spacey emphasized one particular trait that is not always associated with artists, and too seldom associated with entrepreneurs, yet, this trait is essential to success in both art and business ...

... Courage.

Artistic courage is the courage to express your ideas to the world. It's the courage to innovate, to push the boundaries and explore new opportunities for expression.

It might seem this type of courage is the least risky of all the different types of courage, but in many ways it's the most difficult.

Would you run into a burning building to save a small child? Most people say they would—without even thinking about it.

Those same people may find it very difficult to expose his or her personal ideas and thoughts to the scrutiny of the world.

"I find it interesting that in polls the fear of public speaking always trumps the fear of death." It may be that most of us don't have to face death as often as we have to face the specter of speaking in front of a crowd, and whenever we do, we expose ourselves to public scrutiny and criticism—maybe even ridicule.

However, what is business if not the generation of new ideas, products and services—and the process of exposing those ideas to the market?

Not only do you have to blow your own horn to succeed, you've got to do it in front of other people!

The public is inundated with a variety and volume of choices that couldn't even be imagined 5 or 10 years ago.

Whether you run a neighborhood sandwich shop or a multi-national corporation, entrepreneurs with the courage and vision to create, innovate and promote themselves will survive—and some of those will prosper. *Those who don't have artistic courage—won't.*

It *is* scary to expose a new idea to the market—after all, you can do all the market research, analytics and assessments in the world, but you can't know with certainty whether or not the public will accept your new idea until you have the courage to get it out there.

It's natural and it's completely rational to fear that the public or the market might not buy in to what you're putting out there—and it sucks when they don't!

But remember—courage is doing what needs to be done in spite of your fear.

You need to develop the courage to expose your own ideas

or vision both internally to your organization and followers, and externally if that idea is brought to market. You also need the courage to trust, support and encourage the creative minds in your organization—especially when they're struggling to find that next great innovation.

I remember hearing that Bill Gates encouraged his creative teams to produce at least 9 failures a year. He wasn't encouraging purposeful failure, recklessness or foolishness. He simply knew from experience that it took about 9 failures to produce that one remarkable innovation that was going to really change the landscape.

The leader walks a tightrope between managing failures and encouraging risk taking. It's part of your role to support your people in calculated risk. It's also vital that you don't discourage them or worse, scare them away from the creative process.

What happens when the leader creates fear and trepidation when it comes to innovation and change?

How creative will your people be when they're constantly expecting the ax to fall?

How creative would YOU be under those conditions?

Your job is not to intimidate, terrify or discourage followers. Your job is to give them opportunities to develop and test their abilities.

It's your job to support them as they take the risks needed to create, innovate and advance the organization.

It requires courage to expose your ideas to the public. A failed artistic endeavor or business decision will rarely cost you your life, but you do sometimes risk your reputation, career, legacy and, in business, your life savings.

But artistic courage is not about playing it safe—it's about being bold. That's what gets you to the top—and what keeps you there.

CONFIDENCE, UNCERTAINTY AND COURAGE — A STRANGE BUT NECESSARY COMBINATION

Confidence and courage are inseparable. You've got to study and understand the relationship between the two.

Confidence is one of the most important qualities you must develop if you want to accomplish anything meaningful. You must develop confidence if you want others to trust and follow you willingly.

The major problem with confidence is that people confuse it with certainty.

Confidence is NOT absolute certainty! At least it's not surety in a specific outcome.

DEVELOP A HEALTHY RELATIONSHIP WITH UNCERTAINTY

Don't avoid uncertainty. The best leaders accept it, just as they do fear. Uncertainty is an opportunity to test your ingenuity, creativity and adaptability under pressure. One old saying goes, *"The warrior is only truly tested in battle."*

In their article, "Acceptance of Uncertainty as an Indicator of Effective Leadership," Randall White and Sandra Shullman of Executive Development Group expand the importance of a leader's ability to handle uncertainty:

> ... we suggest that being an effective leader is contingent on the ability to deal with ambiguity and its resulting cognitive-affective reaction, uncertainty. Those who can keep the experience of uncertainty to a tolerable level can keep more options open and embrace ambiguity as an opportunity to bring people and options together to learn and adapt collectively as they find their way.

In life and business, as in battle, you just can't guarantee any particular outcome with absolute certainty. There are too many variables, and it's impossible to predict or anticipate every possibility.

The effective leader responds to uncertainty, to changing conditions and circumstances by adapting.

Back to General Patton ...

> One does not plan and then try to make circumstances fit those plans. One tries to make plans fit the circumstances. I think the difference between success and failure in high command depends upon the ability, or lack of it, to do just that.

You *can* guarantee how diligently you train and prepare

yourself to handle unanticipated situations. You have complete control over your preparation.

The better you train and plan, the more likely you are to perform well under fire. Training and preparation cultivate the genuine confidence to face any given challenge with the absolute certainty that you've done everything you can to assure your best performance in that moment ...

... *win, lose or draw.*

That's why genuinely confident people can walk away from a defeat ready to pick themselves up, dust themselves off and start all over again.

Confidence is the mother of perseverance!

This is critical. Leaders are often forged through failure and disaster.

Leaders are those people who display the courage to keep moving when the situation is most desperate or difficult.

This is type of courage is essential to the entrepreneurial leader. Thomas Edison showed this type of courage. Facing failure after endless failure, critics attacked Edison as either foolish or just plain incompetent. His answer:

"I HAVE NOT FAILED; I'VE JUST FOUND 10,000 WAYS THAT DIDN'T WORK."

Confidence is one of the most attractive characteristics of a leader. Genuine confidence, tempered with humility, will make you an effective person—and an effective leader at any level.

Genuine confidence will help you attract loyal and enthusiastic followers whether you hold a position of authority or command, or you stand shoulder to shoulder with your troops in the trenches.

The subject of confidence and its relationship to courage is intensely personal to me. When I finally decided to walk up those dojo stairs to learn how to become a fighter, I was still a broken person. I had absolutely no sense of confidence.

I can't help feeling now, as I did then, that when I was an addict—I was a coward.

I'm not putting down people with addictions. I'm just acknowledging the truth that an addiction is very often an escape from something painful—fear, doubt, even self-loathing.

Drugs, alcohol and other addictions provide a sanctuary from pain, stress, pressure and whatever monsters you see in your mind, or your mirror.

An addict doesn't face those challenges—an addict runs from them.

I can identify with Edison. It took me about 10,000 attempts to find my light too—and I found mine in the dojo.

The light I was looking for was confidence.

I knew instinctively that I couldn't do anything meaningful in my life without it.

One of the best moments in my life was the day I earned my Black Belt ...

Believe me, I knew I had a long way to go, and I know I still have, but earning that belt helped me see what I had become and helped me appreciate the transformation I'd made to that point.

The test only lasts a few hours, but you don't earn a Black Belt by passing a single test. You earn it over years of training and practice.

In martial arts, we call this process Kung Fu.

Ultimately, the belt itself is just a symbol. Tying a black belt around your waist doesn't give you any kind of superhuman power. The belt doesn't somehow endow you with confidence and courage.

Tying on your belt for the first time is special, but it's the journey that matters. The belt represents that journey, and every one of those thousand miles in Lao Tzu's proverb. It's along that journey that we develop our skills, talents and abilities, and most of all—that's where we develop our confidence.

CONFIDENCE IS NOT A VACCINE AGAINST DOUBT

When I started, I didn't know if I was going to make it to Black Belt. I almost quit several times along the way. For every success, I had many more moments of self-doubt, fear and insecurity.

What I learned on that journey is that I could face this doubt and fear.

I learned that I could survive setbacks and disappointments and keep moving forward.

I learned that I could face all these things without drugs. I had something better now, something positive instead of destructive—my workouts were infusing me with confidence.

Even so—on the day of my Black Belt test I had my doubts. During my test there were moments when I didn't think I could do one more push-up, throw one more kick, or take one more fall. Hell, I didn't even think I was passing through most of the test!

What I did know that day was that I had done everything I could possibly do to prepare for that test.

Believe me, I wanted that belt. I would have been terribly disappointed if I didn't get it. But I also knew that whether or not I made it, I could walk away knowing I'd done my best.

That was the first time in my life I knew what true confidence felt like.

That was a significant turning point in my life.

When I earned my Black Belt, I became serious about teaching and about becoming a professional martial artist. I shifted my focus in life toward opening my own dojo. I wanted to become the leader of my own business and my own community of students.

The Black Belt is a symbol of many things and is certainly a symbol of leadership.

Accepting my Black Belt that day did not suddenly turn me into a leader. The process of earning my belt helped prepare me to accept leadership responsibilities. That process became an important part of my transformation from loser to leader.

You cannot guarantee an outcome, but you can guarantee that you've prepared yourself to give your best when you face your toughest challenges.

That's what courage is all about.

COMPASSION

The good folks at Gallup asked 10,000 people what qualities they want and feel are most important in leaders.

No big surprises—here's what they want:

COMPASSION
  TRUST
  STABILITY
  HOPE

People want leaders who care about them.

People respond much better, work harder, produce more and create more new ideas when they know that their leaders care.

When people have faith in leadership, they're more ambitious, courageous and innovative. They're more loyal, vested and committed.

The Sensei Leader practices caring in the form of sincere compassion and empathy. It's leadership on a personal level—an intimate level. This is exactly what people all over the world want and need from their leaders—and it's nothing new.

About 2500 years ago, Sun Tzu wrote in *The Art of War:*

"**R**EGARD YOUR SOLDIERS AS YOUR
CHILDREN, AND THEY WILL FOLLOW
YOU INTO THE DEEPEST VALLEYS;
LOOK ON THEM AS YOUR OWN BELOVED
SONS, AND THEY WILL STAND BY YOU
EVEN UNTO DEATH."

Hopefully you don't have to take it that far—but you get the point!

COMPASSION—NOT WEAKNESS...

Compassion just might be the single most misunderstood characteristic of leadership.

Compassion is not weakness.

Genuine compassion is an expression of strength.

Compassion goes much deeper than just being kind.

Compassion is genuine empathy, a sincere, mindful attempt to understand the feelings, needs and desires of others.

If you want to be an effective leader, compassion involves developing a meaningful and authentic connection with the needs, desires and motivations of your followers.

It's not always easy to see things from the other person's perspective, especially when you're busy or you have operational duties to worry about. It is, however, your responsibility as a leader to do just that—another important lesson taught to me by a very young student ...

This kid was only about 10 years old, but he was a serious student who always worked hard—except for this one day.

My apologies—I can't remember his name. Let's just call him Bobby.

It wasn't that he was being a wise-guy or acting out—he was just having a bad day—moving slow—not paying attention.

Sometimes all it takes is one lazy kid to bring down the energy of the entire class, so I pushed him a bit.

I yelled, *"Let's go! Get it together!* Are you going to be this lazy if an attacker jumps you?" You know, standard Sensei banter.

Bobby seemed to be on another planet. He wasn't keeping pace with the other kids during drills and it finally got to the point where I thought he was going to get hurt, or hurt someone else.

I'd had enough.

"Bobby—*that's it!* Sit down until you can get your head in the game!"

I was admittedly short tempered that day—it happens to the best of us. Still, even when I've got my undies in a twist I always make sure I follow a strict protocol. Whenever I have to sit a student out, I always go over and ask one question:

"Why are you sitting here?"

Many times the kid will say, "Because—*you told me to!"*

Wrong answer!

Anyway—all I'm trying to do with that question is to get the kid to think a little bit about his actions and hopefully take some responsibility.

I knelt on the floor next to Bobby, arms crossed, and said:

"You know, you're usually one of the best kids on the floor. You're one of the best martial artists we've got! What the heck is going on today?"

"Well," he answered, "my grandmother died today."

Well who was the jerk now?

All I could say was, "Geez Bobby, I'm sorry to hear that. Why don't you jump back in class and do the best you can?"

A few minutes later his Mom arrived to pick him up. After I told her what happened, she apologized and said, "I wanted to give you a heads-up, but I couldn't get in touch with you in time."

I asked why Bobby was even in class today given everything that was going on at home.

She explained that the house was pretty chaotic with family and friends coming and going. She thought it would be best for Bobby to keep his routine as normal as possible.

Then she pushed the knife all the way in:

"Bobby just loves you so much—he wanted to be with you today."

I share this story every time I train new instructors and

very often in my workshops for business leaders. The point is—I made some assumptions before I knew what was going on.

I was looking at the situation from only my perspective. I was more concerned with the smooth operation of the class than I was about understanding what was obviously anomalous behavior on the part of one of my best students.

I could have—and should have—taken the time to ask a couple of questions before I responded out of frustration and anger.

I could have taken a much more compassionate approach.

DON'T CONFUSE EMPATHY AND SYMPATHY

Another problem is the semantic confusion between empathy and sympathy. These are two very different concepts.

Sympathy refers to agreement with or a sense of harmony with the thoughts and feelings of someone else.

Empathy is nothing of the kind.

Empathy is the act of understanding another person's thoughts and feelings—whether you agree with them or not.

Empathy refers to the proverbial act of walking a mile in someone else's shoes before judging.

It takes strength and courage to pause, especially under stress, and take the time to truly understand another person's point of view.

No one would accuse Sun Tzu of being a pacifist, yet in *The Art of War* he teaches us to become *"one with the enemy."*

Sun Tzu talks about understanding the mind of the enemy—empathy:

IF YOU KNOW THE ENEMY AND KNOW YOURSELF, YOU NEED NOT FEAR THE RESULT OF A HUNDRED BATTLES.

IF YOU KNOW YOURSELF BUT NOT THE ENEMY, FOR EVERY VICTORY GAINED YOU WILL ALSO SUFFER A DEFEAT.

IF YOU KNOW NEITHER THE ENEMY NOR YOURSELF, YOU WILL SUCCUMB IN EVERY BATTLE.

He's not describing a sympathetic position. Sun Tzu is talking about the strategic importance of knowing your enemy as completely as you can.

He also points out the shortcoming in the egotistical perspective. Knowing yourself is not enough. You've got to try and understand the other guy.

You gain a great advantage as a leader if you're willing to understand both your own mind and the minds and hearts of your followers, and, of course, your enemies!

Empathy is a very useful quality when you're seeking a resolution to a dispute, problem or challenge:

Can you rise above the din of battle and listen to all sides of the argument from a detached, more objective vantage point?

Can you put aside your personal feelings and emotions long enough to at least listen to different perspectives or points of view?

Dr. Stephen Covey, a more contemporary sage, put it this way:

"SEEK FIRST TO UNDERSTAND."

That's a pretty good working application of empathy.

Conflict can stall or cripple an organization, even a society. Isn't it strange that conflict is most inevitable when you can least afford it, such as when you're preparing to lead a significant change or when the poop is really hitting the fan.

Empathy streamlines resolution.

When you understand the other perspective, your response is more informed and your chosen course of action usually more effective, whether you sympathize with the other guy's perspective or not.

And you may not agree!

Sometimes you do find yourself squared off with a true adversary—an intractable enemy. When there is no clear path to resolution, a thorough knowledge of the mind of your opponent is a tremendous advantage for any effective leader.

More wisdom from Sun Tzu; think about this:

"THE OPPORTUNITY TO SECURE
OURSELVES AGAINST DEFEAT LIES
IN OUR OWN HANDS, BUT THE
OPPORTUNITY OF DEFEATING THE
ENEMY IS PROVIDED BY THE ENEMY
HIMSELF."

In this case, don't mistake my kindness for weakness! In fact, don't even assume I'm being kind. Empathy may simply be my way to discover and exploit your weakness!

IS THE SENSEI A "SERVANT LEADER"?

The theory of "servant leadership" is getting a lot of attention these days.

Service to others is certainly a meaningful expression of compassionate leadership, but don't confuse service with subservience.

The servant leader is still—a leader.

You're not abdicating any responsibility or authority. You're committing your leadership, your talents and skills and whatever authority you possess to serve others.

If you truly want to embrace the ideal of servant leadership—think of yourself as Samurai.

The Samurai of feudal Japan were a caste of warriors who were trained in the ideal that sacrifice to their cause, and to their leader, was their highest calling. The word Samurai literally means: *one who embraces a life of service.*

Putting aside the interesting historical fact that Samurai would commit ritual suicide to preserve their honor should they fail in their duty—their commitment to service still works pretty well today.

JIM BOUCHARD

The most effective leaders understand that leadership is a vocation of *service*—of putting others first—and that sometimes requires great sacrifice.

In **THINK Like a BLACK BELT** I wrote:

> Leadership is not a process of taking. It's a process of giving. Leadership is not the act of exploiting other people for your own ends. It's not the simple acquisition of title or station so you'll enjoy the associated privileges or benefits. Leadership is true sacrifice. A true leader is willing to sacrifice for the benefit of his followers.

Compassion and service are closely related.

Compassionate leadership is not about selfish acquisition. It's not about making yourself more important. It's about understanding the needs of the people who trust and follow you. It's about your responsibility to others, to your followers.

It's not about your followers serving you, it's about you serving them.

If the ideals of the servant leader appeal to you, but the term "servant" seems a little weak or condescending, adopt some symbolism that has a little swagger to it …

… Call yourself Samurai!

102

RESPECT

The defining characteristic of authentic compassion is respect.

Years ago I was asked to speak at an elementary school. The teachers there were impressed with the respectful behavior of my students in school and asked me to talk to the rest of their students about respect and responsibility.

I still do this today whether I'm talking to a group of kids or to C-level executives—I started the talk by asking for a definition of the word *"respect."*

Go ahead and do the same exercise right now. Take just a couple of minutes and try to clearly define the word "respect."

Most people have some gut level understanding of the word. They know it when they see it, they know when it's not there, but at the same time most people struggle to explain exactly what respect is.

One young man stood up and knocked me completely off my script. This young guy stood up, bowed, and said:

"Sensei—respect means taking care of one another."

You might as well have punched me in the stomach. I literally had to sit down and catch my breath.

Have you ever heard a better definition of the word respect?

Believe me, this was not one of the responses I had prepared for. After gathering my thoughts, I stood up, bowed to this young philosopher, and said:

"Thank you! You are exactly right. Respect is— taking care of one another."

I didn't know it at the time, but this young man's words would change the entire course of my career and life.

I knew in that moment that this message needed to be shared—and not just with people who liked to kick and punch. With the benefit of hindsight I now know that what happened that day started me on the path to becoming a speaker and writer.

Respect means caring for others. Compassion is the means to express caring—respectfully, with the best interests of others in your heart and in your mind, even when it's tough to do.

No—especially when it's tough!

WISDOM

> *"ALL LEADERS ARE ACTUAL OR POTENTIAL*
> *POWER HOLDERS, BUT NOT ALL POWER*
> *HOLDERS ARE LEADERS."*

~JAMES MACGREGOR BURNS

You can use your power to become a tyrant or a leader. The determining factor is—wisdom.

Wisdom is knowledge and experience tempered by awareness.

Most people believe that knowledge itself is power. As a quick aside, most people also believe money is power. Those are two very dangerous beliefs.

If knowledge and money were power in and of themselves, then *all* smart, rich people would be powerful—and *no* stupid or desperate people would be.

Keep in mind that power is simply your ability to perform effectively.

Knowledge is an essential resource for power—you need to be knowledgeable to perform effectively, but it's not enough.

People expect leaders to be knowledgeable. In fact, they usually expect leaders to know more than they do, at least in certain areas—but knowledge alone does not a leader make!

Knowledge is a readily accessible commodity—for the willing. Today there is literally no limit to the knowledge and information you can access from your laptop computer.

You probably know people who are "book smart." They seem to suck up knowledge like sponges, but they never seem to do anything with it.

A leader can't rely on book smarts. You need to develop a deeper process, the ability to transform knowledge into something much more meaningful, something that can be expressed and shared and can transform lives.

That something is wisdom.

You develop wisdom by taking what you know and doing something with it. This means seeking out new challenges and new adventures, new opportunities to apply your knowledge to produce ever more powerful results.

Knowledge can be acquired. Wisdom is earned.

That means rolling with the punches and learning from mistakes as well as building on success. It also means you've got to discipline yourself to commit serious time and thought to reflection and continual self-assessment.

KNOWLEDGE WITHOUT EXPERIENCE AND AWARENESS CAN BE EXTREMELY DANGEROUS

In the martial arts I've met several 20 year-old "masters." These guys have the knowledge and the technical skill to pass a test and get a certificate and a title, but they really don't have the life experience and wisdom to bear the responsibility that comes with being an authentic Master.

I'm sure you've known people like that in life and in business, too. They seem to know-it-all, but they've lived very little. These people seldom have the experience or credibility that earns loyalty and trust. They haven't yet developed the steely nerved calm and reserve that puts followers at ease in the face of adversity.

No matter how much you know, people will not follow you unless you can demonstrate the experience and awareness necessary to apply that knowledge effectively—in a way that demonstrates your wisdom and inspires others with a true sense of trustworthiness, meaning and purpose.

That's the wisdom of the genuine leader.

AWARENESS: THE TRANSCENDENT QUALITY OF WISDOM

Nearly every day in the dojo, I played a game with my junior students …

I would yell, *"What are the two most important words in the martial arts?"*

They would shout:

"PAY—ATTENTION!"

That's what awareness is in a nutshell—your ability to pay attention.

"Pay attention" are the two most important words in real life and business too. Awareness is the process that tempers knowledge and experience into wisdom. Awareness is an essential ingredient if you want to access your peak levels of performance as a leader and as a person.

You've got to develop this awareness in two-dimensions, external and internal. You've got to pay attention to what's happening around you, and what's happening within you.

External awareness is relatively easy—once you master the internal.

The process of self-discovery, of continual learning and development, requires a great deal of focus and discipline. It requires an abandonment of the ego and a willingness to undergo constant introspection and self-analysis.

Anyone can become more aware, if they're willing. One of the most distinguishing traits of a leader is the willingness to embrace this process.

Most people simply won't.

I believe most people shy away from this process because it can be difficult and painful work, much like earning a Black Belt—but it's not complicated.

THE ONLY TOOL YOU NEED TO GET STARTED—A MIRROR

I told you about my past life as a drug addict. I told you about the times I was literally facing myself in my bathroom mirror. I absolutely hated what I saw.

I also saw my reflection in a mirror the first day I opened my martial arts center.

We usually install a wall of mirrors in the dojo so students can see what they're doing as they practice. On this first day, of course, I was the only one in the building.

109

I wanted to make sure I looked the part, so I put on my uniform and stepped in front of the mirror to tie my belt.

I have to admit, I spent a few minutes just looking at myself. I was, for one of the first times in my life—genuinely proud.

What I saw in the mirror this day was much different than the reflection from my drug days.

From then on, clear sailing—right? Of course not!

Over the years I faced many challenges. I still do—and I expect to face many more. What was different that day was that I felt ready for these challenges.

I understood myself on a much deeper level. I understood the process of awareness. I knew that I would examine and challenge myself as much as, if not more than anyone else would.

I also knew that from then on, I could accept whatever reflection I saw in the mirror—and that I could always grow from there.

Whether you take this practice literally or metaphorically, you've got to find some way and commit some time to look in the mirror once in a while. You've got to think clearly about what you see there. You've got to decide whether that reflection represents who and what you truly want to be at any given time, or you've got to reflect on what you want to change—and how.

Awareness is the practice of assessing who and where you

are—right here and right now. It's the practice of paying attention and understanding the circumstances and conditions you are experiencing—right here and right now.

It's also kind of an inventory. What material, emotional and spiritual resources do you have at your disposal—right here and right now?

On its highest level, awareness is understanding others and your relationship to the people around you. After all, your life is a human experience largely defined by your relationships with other human beings.

Awareness is your ability to experience life here and now.

The past and future are important too, but you can't do a damn thing about your history or your dreams, except by what you do—*right here and right now.*

The ancient masters taught us that the only thing that lasts forever is the present moment. The past is done and the future hasn't arrived yet. You make amends for the past and you shape your future in the present. Awareness is your ability to be open to this present moment.

I said that external awareness is relatively simple once you master the internal process. I can sum it all up in another game I still play when I teach kids …

I yell, *"Eyes?"*

They yell, *"OPEN!"*

"Ears?"

"OPEN!"

"Heart?"

"OPEN!"

"Mind?"

"OPEN!"

"Mouth?"

"CLOSED!!!"

That's the entire formula for awareness.

Now—go look in the mirror!

BEGINNER'S MIND

Wisdom transcends knowledge.

Wisdom is growth. A wise person never stops growing.

When I got my Black Belt, my Master gave me a brand new belt. It was a deep, rich shade of black. It was one of the most beautiful things I had ever seen.

He told me that if I continued my life as a martial artist, I would tie and untie that belt thousands of times. I'd be dragged around the floor in it. Over the years that belt would be drenched in buckets of blood and sweat—and even a few tears.

Eventually, he said, that belt would start to fade and wear out. That deep black outer-layer of fabric would fray and tear away. I knew exactly what he was talking about.

Our belts wear out as time goes on. The black covering frays exposing another belt at the core. Underneath the black cover, the belt is white—the color of our very first rank.

This reminds us to keep what we call—

"Beginner's Mind."

Beginner's Mind is an enthusiastic sense of wonder and curiosity. It means approaching each new day as an opportunity to learn, grow and develop.

You see—the mind of the true Master is really the mind of the beginner.

Wisdom is not a static state—it's an ever-expanding cycle of discovery. That's why it's so important to keep our hunger for new learning alive and well fed.

Our worn out, threadbare belts might tell others that we've been around a while. They remind us that no matter how far we've traveled, there is always another journey ahead.

One of the Masters I admired most was Professor Nick Cerio. Professor Cerio taught that the true meaning of the Black Belt was simply the development of good learning attitude.

By earning a Black Belt, you learn how to learn.

The Professor's belt was worn to a thread.

One day I heard someone joke with the Professor saying, "Hey Professor, when are you going to get a new belt?"

He shot back, *"Never!* They'll put me in the box with this one!"

As far as I know, they did.

The Professor was a very wise man.

PART THREE
STRATEGIES AND TACTICS

8 STRATEGIES OF THE SENSEI LEADER

"STUDY STRATEGY OVER THE YEARS AND ACHIEVE THE SPIRIT OF THE WARRIOR. TODAY IS VICTORY OVER YOURSELF OF YESTERDAY; TOMORROW IS YOUR VICTORY OVER LESSER MEN."

~MIYAMOTO MUSASHI

Musashi is the iconic face of Japan's legendary sword heritage. His legacy is a book commonly known as *The Book of Five Rings,* which has become one of the most respected books on strategy ever written and is required reading in business and leadership studies around the world.

We don't live in feudal Japan, and I doubt Musashi could have imagined the challenges we face in our times.

We've never enjoyed so much freedom, yet we've never been more willing to surrender our freedom for the illusion of safety and security.

Our expectations have never been greater.

Our basic human needs remain the same, but the levels we feel obligated to reach in order to feel satisfied have never been higher.

Technology and instant global communication have changed the way we connect and do business with people all over the world.

These new times require a new type of leader—a new type of leader that understands some very old strategies of leadership.

Today's leader must be tomorrow's leader—respectful of the past with a clear vision for the future.

I've taken the lessons I've learned over 30 years of practice and study and condensed them down to 8 basic strategies for effective leadership.

I believe Musashi would recognize some of them:

1) NEVER LIMIT YOURSELF TO ONE LEADERSHIP STYLE.

2) BE TOUGH, YET COMPASSIONATE.

3) BE A JACK OF ALL TRADES, MASTER OF ONE OR TWO.

4) BE CONFIDENT, YET HUMBLE— LEAD BY EXAMPLE.

5) BE FLEXIBLE, ADAPTABLE AND COMFORTABLE WITH UNCERTAINTY.

6) BE A SKILLED COMMUNICATOR.

7) BE A DEDICATED TEACHER, COACH AND MENTOR.

8) LEAD BY SHARING, NOT BY ACCUMULATING.

Now I'm sure you could add more items to these *8 Strategies,* but the point is not to make it more complicated, but to find the most essential things you must do consistently to attract, serve and maintain a strong base of loyal and willing followers.

The Masters I admire most are reductionists. They operate on the principle that all complex systems and processes are simply combinations of actionable steps and basic techniques.

Let's keep it as simple as we can.

1. NEVER LIMIT YOURSELF TO ONE LEADERSHIP STYLE

Be articulate in a number of styles and be able to apply the appropriate style to specific circumstances and conditions.

How many Black Belts does it take to screw in a light bulb?

A hundred.

One to actually perform the operation, and 99 others to brag about how they would have it done it better.

Substitute leadership experts for black belts in this joke and you'll need to multiply by 1,000.

The absolute last thing this world needs is another leadership style. We've got plenty of leadership experts, and it seems as if every few weeks, one of them develops a new style, method, or theory, heralded as revolutionary, that every leader must adopt immediately—or they're doomed.

Today's leader cannot be limited by one style.

First of all, no one style works in every application. Our age of nearly borderless global trade and interaction exposes cultural differences that should make it obvious that a leadership style rooted in one culture can rarely if ever be effectively transplanted to another without compromise or modification.

Even within the same organization, you may be leading a group made up of individuals with a wide variety of cultural backgrounds and experiences.

Geert Hofstede, the founder of the Institute for Research on Intercultural Cooperation has studied the leadership styles in countries all over the world. If anyone would have the qualifications to identify a unified theory of leadership, it might be Hofstede, but he writes; "I am not offering a solution; I only protest against a naive universalism that knows only one recipe for development."

No—there is no unified theory in leadership.

The natural ethnocentric tendency is to assume that the style that works best in your own culture among your own people might work everywhere else, or with everyone else.

Not so much.

Today's leader must be open minded, well informed and ready to integrate various styles and techniques to the task and the people at hand.

THE MOST EFFECTIVE MARTIAL ARTISTS ARE THIEVES

Leaders should be thieves, too, at least when it comes to adapting styles and techniques.

The best martial artists don't rely on one particular style or method. We steal techniques whenever and wherever we can to become more powerful, effective and efficient fighters. We study any number of different styles and methods, taking the best from each to develop a wide range of skills and techniques adaptable to changing conditions and situations.

Bruce Lee had this advice for martial artists:

"IN PRIMARY FREEDOM, ONE UTILIZES ALL WAYS AND IS BOUND BY NONE, AND LIKEWISE USES ANY TECHNIQUES OR MEANS WHICH SERVES ONE'S END."

Lee's advice works just as well for leaders.

Apply this mindset to leadership, and it looks a lot like what the academics call *"flex leadership," "consequential"* or *"situational"* styles. This means adapting your methodology to the particular situation at hand and being adaptable to the conditions and circumstances you face in any given moment.

We have an old fortune cookie saying in martial arts:

"THERE ARE ONLY TWO TECHNIQUES. THE ONE THAT WORKS AND THE ONE THAT DOESN'T."

In any given moment there are only two options in regard

to leadership style—the one that will work and the one that won't.

The fastest and surest way to find the technique that won't work is to be inflexible or dogmatic, to limit yourself to one particular style or technique.

In the dojo and in business, these limitations are often an unintended consequence of tradition. Too many organizations and leaders restrict innovation and retard effectiveness because of historical inertia.

I found this gem on *LinkedIn:*

WHAT IS THE GREATEST BARRIER TO GROWTH AND PROGRESS?

THE WORDS: WE'VE ALWAYS DONE IT THAT WAY.

Tradition is important, but tradition should inform, not limit our response to current circumstances and conditions.

Learn from past tradition and styles, but also be open to advancing those styles when you can, adapting them to new times, needs, and opportunities. Be willing to discard anything that just doesn't work anymore.

You honor tradition by borrowing the best of it, not by hanging yourself with it.

LEADERSHIP STYLES

Become articulate in a number of styles and techniques so you can skillfully apply the techniques and theories that fit the situation.

Modern martial artists borrow a lot from the ancient Japanese *"Budo,"* or Way of the Warrior.

A Samurai warrior could increase his value by learning various war crafts and skills. A leader becomes more effective by studying a wide range of leadership styles and by incorporating the techniques and methods of effective leaders from the past and from today's leadership innovators.

One of the earliest attempts in the modern study of leadership comes from the work of psychologist Kurt Lewin. He divided leadership into 3 major styles:

- **Authoritarian**
- **Participative**
- **Delegative**

Most contemporary leadership theories fit into one or more of these three major styles.

As the name implies, *authoritarian styles,* sometimes called *autocratic,* are the command and control theories of leadership.

Participative or *democratic leadership* encourages a more synergistic approach where the leader and followers work cooperatively.

Don't worry—in these styles the leader still retains the final say in all major decisions.

Delegative or *laissez faire* style allows for the greatest degree of autonomy for followers.

Be careful, this style can sometimes provide cover for a lazy or complacent manager who isn't capable or simply doesn't want to make tough decisions. Be *very* careful you do not use delegation as a means to avoid tough decisions or skirt responsibility.

Experts have battled for the past 60 years over which style is most effective or productive. The truth is that each and every style can work well when matched with the right situation, circumstances and conditions.

Effective leaders know how to apply the appropriate style, theory or technique to the situation.

Stylistic differences are always a ready point of contention between martial artists too. We very often get calls from martial artists who are, for a variety of reasons, changing either schools or instructors. One of the first questions they'll ask is, "How is your style different than mine?"

One of my co-founders at Northern Chi used to have a great response this question.

Jim Ambrose Sensei would ask, "Do you punch in your system?"

The caller would answer, "Sure!"

Then Jim Sensei would say, "Yeah, we punch here too! You kick over there?"

"Of course!"

Then Jim would answer:

"Yeah, we kick here too!"

He could keep this up for quite a while. His point was that similarities between styles usually far outweigh the differences.

In martial arts, the goal of any style is to become more powerful, to kick, punch and dispatch your opponent as effectively as possible and to realize your full potential as a fighter.

The leader's goal is to become more powerful, too. In leadership, this means serving your people as effectively as you can to inspire their best efforts and cultivate the success of the organization.

Almost any system, style or theory can be applied effectively if you apply that style to the appropriate situation. The trick is to understand the strengths and weaknesses of each.

Leadership theory has evolved quite over the past few years. Academics today identify several major theories:

THE GREAT MAN THEORY

This theory started the endless war over whether leaders are born or made.

I'll end the debate—and quickly.

There are no born leaders.

This is the one theory you can throw out right now.

Most credible experts have abandoned this tired idea.

Some people can, however, by accident of birth, start with favorable conditions that can make it more likely that they'll develop into leaders.

You can find some compelling examples that might make it look like the *Great Man Theory* still holds water.

The Kennedy brothers, Teddy Roosevelt and George S. Patton were born into families with every favorable condition for the incubation of leaders, particularly a family culture and tradition—even an expectation that anyone born to their stock would become leaders.

If you know science, however, you know that you only need one black swan to disprove the theory that all swans are white.

In each of these legendary families, you also find misfits, miscreants and failures.

Look into the lives of the examples I chose, and you'll find remarkable flaws in each of these individuals. Any one of them could have as easily ended up in jail, in the Hall of Shame, or relegated to obscurity instead of ensconced in the pantheon of iconic leadership.

For the *Great Man Theory* to hold up, you'd also have to overlook the many stories of leaders who rise to the highest levels from the most improbable circumstances. Here you'll find Abe Lincoln, Mahatma Ghandi and even Bill Clinton.

You'd also find those people who had never held positions of authority, rank or title, but who became iconic leaders when faced with unusual circumstances and remarkable challenges. Rosa Parks, Louis Zamperini, Maya Angelou and

Martin Luther King—these people weren't born to the circumstances that breed leaders. They rose to leadership because they found themselves in that time and place where leaders are called—and they answered.

These people don't usually aspire to positions of authority; more often than not they'd rather go about their business without fanfare, but by example they inspire and influence many followers.

The idea of the born leader is a myth, and one that needs to be busted.

Leaders can be trained despite the most improbable conditions of birth, and people born with a silver leadership spoon in their mouths do not realize their potential without training, practice and opportunity.

TRAIT THEORY

Trait Theory is an extension of the born or made debate—but in my opinion, a little more useful.

Some people are born with traits that would seem to predispose them to become natural leaders. For example, strange as it might seem, research shows that tall people tend to attract more followers than short people. However, there are plenty of noted leaders who were not tall. Napoleon of course comes to mind, but there are plenty of other leaders who for different reasons do not fit societal norms for physical attractiveness.

Personality traits such as charisma, confidence, empathy and likability can often overcome any societal shortcomings in regard to physical traits. We can identify and emulate these behavioral traits—at least to some extent.

SKILLS THEORY

Somewhat related to *Trait Theory* in that specific skills, technical, interpersonal and conceptual skills can be cultivated and developed.

This is where you'll find the critical mass of contemporary study and practice that focuses on emulating the skills of people who have proven themselves to be effective leaders.

To be a good leader, all you have to do, is do what they do—right?

At first glance, *Skills Theory* seems to fit nicely in the idea of The Sensei Leader, but be careful. Keep remembering not to limit yourself to any one style—or any one particular skill.

SITUATIONAL, STYLE, OR BEHAVIORAL THEORIES

Each of these theories allows for leadership to be developed—and for effective leaders to adapt to some degree to the situation or conditions they face.

CONTINGENCY THEORY

The leader is chosen to fit the situation.

Contingency Theory addresses the problem that not all leaders or leadership styles work effectively with all cultures, needs or situations. It also addresses the fact that situations and conditions change continually.

With *Contingency Theory,* instead of retraining leaders in a new style, you install a leader who brings a developed style that fits the present conditions.

Moving on, you have what I see as largely variations on the *developmental* leadership theories …

TRANSACTIONAL AND MANAGEMENT THEORIES

These theories lean heavily on the relationship between incentive and motivation.

You manage and control processes, systems and conditions in an attempt to incentivize and reward high performance, and reduce or punish failure.

TRANSFORMATIONAL THEORY

Transformational Theory depends on a leaders ability to inspire others and cultivate and develop their talents and abilities.

This leads us to …

RELATIONSHIP THEORIES, MENTORING THEORIES AND OF COURSE, SERVANT LEADERSHIP

This group is rooted in the belief that you bring out the best in followers by nurturing, mentoring and supporting individual growth and development.

These theories emphasize the importance of interpersonal skills and emotional intelligence. The leaders that operate under these theories focus on building trust and emotional capital.

OK, so which of these styles and theories best fits The Sensei Leader?

Except for "The Great Man Theory"—all of them!

If you really want to pin me down, I'd place a little more weight on the situational, transformational and service theories.

Just don't exclude anything that might work. Be a jack of all trades—and master of one or two!

I lean a little heavier on the side of situational and transformational leadership because of the emphasis on adaptability and responsiveness to changing conditions and needs, and because of their focus on the human aspects of leadership.

Paul Hersey and Kenneth Blanchard are noted for their development of what they've actually trademarked as "Situational Leadership®." Here they are as quoted in *The Leader's Companion* by J. Thomas Wren:

Effective leaders need to be able to adapt their chosen style to fit the requirements of the situation. Therefore, the leader must not only know when to use a particular style, but also know how to make each style fit into the situation in order to maximize the performance of subordinates.

Learn as much as you can about each of these styles and theories. Learn where each is effective and where each falls short.

Test them, practice and learn which styles, theories and techniques best fit you and the circumstances and conditions you face as a leader.

The academic debate over a "best" theory is no more useful than a bunch of second grade school kids arguing over who has the best marbles. It's much more useful to learn as much as you can about the leaders you admire.

Understand the conditions they lived with.

Study how they adapted to changing circumstances and how they faced challenges.

Emulate the leaders you admire most ...

... all the while developing your ability to adapt, create and innovate new responses to the challenges and opportunities you face today—and those you'll face in the future.

2. BE TOUGH—
YET COMPASSIONATE

Now let's talk about "tough" compassion.

I said it earlier and I'll say it again—with emphasis:

Genuine compassion is not weakness.

Genuine compassion requires strength and courage. It goes much deeper than being kind—or doing unto others ...

Sometimes compassion is expressed as kindness. At other times it means doing what is right and best—even when that means you've got to be tough, direct, honest and sometimes even cruel.

The general may order 100 troops into a hopeless battle to cover the retreat of 10,000 other men.

Is that decision cruel—or compassionate?

An executive may have to approve the lay-off of 50 loyal employees to save the company and the jobs of 500 others.

Again, cruel or compassionate?

Leaders constantly face difficult choices. Sometimes the most compassionate choice may not be the kindest—at least on first glance.

COMPASSION AND BAD BEHAVIOR

One problem area that comes up frequently in my workshops is the issue of confronting bad actors in your organization.

It may seem like the more compassionate course is to give someone the benefit of the doubt when they're behaving badly—quite the opposite. Failure to honor your standards and failure to hold people accountable can in fact be a gross display of weakness, maybe even cowardice.

My dear friend and mentor Larry Winget wrote this in his best-selling book, *Grow A Pair:*

> Many workers come to work late, put in just enough work to get by, and have little respect for their co-workers or management and even less respect for their customers. They figure that management and the HR department wouldn't risk a lawsuit and they think they can get by with damn near any type of poor behavior without any consequences.

Larry has a tough solution for lousy employees:

> Grow a pair! Fire every employee who gives you less than you pay them for. Stop tolerating poor performance in every single employee down to the smallest violation. No more coming in late, no more long lunch hours, and no more half-assed effort in exchange for full pay ...

> Take your business back from the lousy, disinterested employees and put it in the hands of those who care about serving the customer, deliver excellence in all they do, and understand the concept of adding value to your company through hard work.

Cold? Lacking compassion?

Hardly.

When you tolerate bad behavior you are not showing compassion at all—you are a coward.

Your refusal to confront bad actors shows complete disregard, even gross contempt for the people who genuinely value and trust your leadership.

The worst examples of tolerance for bad behavior are those involving harassment and bullying.

You may think you're acting compassionately when you give someone the benefit of the doubt, and you should certainly give anyone accused of these violations a fair hearing, but allowing this type of behavior is inexcusable and can be not only expensive for you—but dangerous to the people involved.

Ashley Alford was an employee of Aaron's Rents in Fairview Heights, Illinois. Richard Moore was her supervisor.

The harassment started with a series of off-color remarks and pet names. It ended in a brutal assault in which Moore held Alford down and masturbated on her.

A federal court awarded Ashley a record $95 million.

It's impossible to protect everyone you serve from the spontaneous actions of any particular individual, but in this case and others like it, leadership certainly is certainly responsible in no small part.

The victim in this case reported the first incidents of harassment. She reported early and often.

According to her official complaint, Ashley contacted her District Supervisor, Brad Markin, who was directly responsible for Moore.

Markin's response was simply to warn Moore to "watch his back" as he had a sexual harassment complaint filed against him.

Was this supervisor acting *compassionately?*

According to reports, Markin was friends with Moore and was likely giving him a chance to change his behavior instead of putting him on the street. *How compassionate was that decision from Ashley Alford's perspective?*

Still think it's compassionate to put up with a bad actor?

Too many times bad behavior is tolerated because the perpetrator is a top performer or even a supervisor, as in the Aaron's Rental example.

Tolerating bad behavior, whatever the justification in your mind, is just plain wrong, and it can be devastating to the people you serve and to your organization.

The only way you demonstrate true compassion to the people you serve is to be tough on bad actors. That is your responsibility as a leader …

… Nobody said it was going to be easy!

COMPASSIONATE CRITICISM

The next conflict between cruel and kind is in delivering honest and sincere criticism.

Sometimes it's not possible or appropriate to "soften the blow." You don't have be rude, and it's usually best to keep your cool under pressure, but to be truly compassionate you must also be frank and direct.

It might feel cruel when you have to call someone on the carpet, but it just might be the best thing you can do for that person in the long run. What looks and feels cruel or unfair might just be a great act of compassion that may even save a life or a career.

In one of my past lives I was writing and producing television commercials at a network affiliate. My supervisor was someone everyone in the office considered a genuine friend—I certainly did.

It took me by complete surprise during a performance review when Gordon found it necessary to give me a good old fashioned butt whupping.

He stated very plainly that my attitude had become a problem. My work was suffering, and people noticed.

At the time my passion was music, and Gordon was extremely supportive of me in that pursuit. On weekends, he worked as a sound tech for my band and he often cleared us to use station equipment and facilities to produce videos after hours.

I was too young and stupid to see how good I had it!

I saw my day job as an obstacle.

Gordon pointed out to me that it was my day job that gave me the means to pursue my dreams in music.

My job provided me with a decent salary, most of which I sunk into the music, and nearly unlimited access to tens of thousands of dollars worth of equipment. He also pointed out that it was through my job that I was developing the technical and creative skills I was using to pursue my musical ambitions.

Then he told me in no uncertain terms that unless I changed my attitude and started acting like the person he had hired, I left him no other option—*I'd be fired.*

I went home for the weekend feeling pretty humiliated.

I could have just been angry and resentful, that would have been in keeping with my rebellious mentality at the time, but there was something about the way Gordon handled the situation that inspired me to really think about what had happened.

He had been brutally honest with me—but I knew he cared.

He had been perfectly "tough yet compassionate." I could tell that he didn't want to fire me, even though I had no doubt that he was fully prepared to do just that.

He saw something in me that I could not see for myself—and he showed me genuine respect by being so honest and direct.

After that, I became the model employee. I found a new

appreciation for my job and really enjoyed the rest of my time at the station.

Ironically, a few years later I found myself in Gordon's role as I found myself on the opposite side of the same situation! This time I was the boss—

I gave Gordon a call and told him that I had just given my employee the same kind of review he had given me. It was tough, but I was grateful for having had the experience from the other end. I thanked him for having been so tough and honest with me all those years ago.

He really didn't remember much about the situation, but he did tell me that he wouldn't have fired me. After all, *we were friends!*

I said, "Gordon—Thank God I didn't know that at the time!"

Many times in my career I've had to tell a hopeful student that they were just not ready to test for Black Belt. Believe me, this part of the job sucks!

I appreciate how hard each student works for the opportunity to test for Black Belt, and believe me, if they've made it this far, it was not for lack of effort. Still, there are times that for any number of reasons, a student is just not ready. You may encounter similar situations regarding a promotion or an appointment to a key project.

Would it be compassionate to expose the student to inevitable failure?

It's much more compassionate to be honest, explain where the student is falling short and recommend specific areas for improvement—even though that might my job a bit tougher!

What good would it do to pass a student who isn't up to the standards?

How would that student feel if they knew they didn't deserve the recognition, but I promoted them anyway?

Am I doing my best for that student by shorting them on the full benefits of this experience?

How confident would they be in their skills?

Is that compassionate?

You don't have to be a jerk about it …

Design an experience that helps the person improve. In the dojo, we usually give a pre-test assessment that exposes any weaknesses or deficiencies. Once I'm sure the student knows he's hit a wall, I ask him if he feels ready—or if he thinks he needs more work.

Nearly every single time, that student will either opt out on his own and start preparing for his next opportunity to test or, in some cases, will double his efforts to get ready.

I'm the leader.

It's my responsibility to make sure my people understand my standards.

It's my responsibility to assure that every candidate knows exactly what we expect for a Black Belt performance.

It's also my responsibility to honor those standards and hold students to them.

Ultimately, that is the most caring, and most compassionate thing I can do ...

... as tough as that might be.

3. Commit yourself to personal & professional Mastery

> "The purpose of training is to tighten up the slack, toughen the body, and polish the spirit."
>
> ~Morihei Ueshiba

If you're a leader, people expect you to know what the hell you're doing! They expect you to be good at what you do!

Practice Mastery in your domain. At the same time, acknowledge that you can't do everything yourself. Understand and cultivate the talents and skills of others to realize the full potential of the organization or community.

Effective leaders are committed to personal and professional mastery. They're also dedicated to providing opportunities so that others can develop mastery too.

A while ago I was soaking in the tub watching Dan Pink's TED Talk on *"The Puzzle of Motivation."* Yeah, that's how I spend my tub time ... YouTube University!

Anyway, Mr. Pink was talking about the three major factors that motivate us:

- **Autonomy**
- **Mastery**
- **Purpose**

His contention is that if you want to engage people—allow them to control how they manage their time and get the job done, provide them with opportunities for growth and development, and make sure they're doing something meaningful.

I think Dan Pink hits the nail squarely on the head.

I'll only add that from my experience, mastery is the most important of these three factors. That's what the Black Belt experience is all about.

Mastery gives you control of your individual talents and abilities. Mastery is the key to self-empowerment.

Mastery is what earns you greater autonomy.

Mastery is in itself a meaningful pursuit—a purpose unto itself.

Mastery is also the foundation of confidence.

You want to feel as if you can accomplish what you set out to do, right?

That confidence comes most of all from training and

preparation—from mastering the talents, skills and abilities you need to accomplish the task at hand and your long term goals.

Mastery, like perfection, is not a destination; it's a process. It's the continual process of learning, training and mindful practice.

You certainly want to master specific skills and abilities—you want to develop your talents and competencies. More important, however, is that you master the process of personal development itself.

It's appropriate to apply the term mastery to a high level of skill and ability in a specific area. The true Master, however, can apply the process of learning to achieve Mastery in any pursuit.

Ultimately, the real secret of Mastery is the ability to master the basics.

MASTERING BASICS

Years ago I attended a session at a martial arts convention featuring the Japanese sword master, Yamazaki. Master Yamazaki had a pedigree including training movie stars and members of the Japanese imperial family—and they take their sword very seriously.

He told a story, mostly through an interpreter, about a young warrior who wanted to become a great sword master.

As these stories go—the young warrior approaches the

Master and says:

"I want to be a great sword master too!"

The Master replies, "You only need to know three steps. First step: Basic practice. Now go away!"

The young man does as he's told and trains diligently for three years. Returning to the Master he announces, "Master, I'm ready for the next step!"

"Good!" says the Master. "Second step: Basic practice! Now go away."

Again the young warrior goes off and trains and practices and duels and tests his skills until he feels he's ready for the final step.

One more time he returns to the Master.

"Master," he says proudly, "I'm ready to become a master, too. I'm ready for the final step."

At this point, Master Yamazaki got his English on and shouted:

"Third step—MORE basic practice! Like Nike! Just do it!"

Basic practice
Basic practice
MORE basic practice!

True Masters in any field are those people who are willing to commit themselves to the difficult, sometimes boring, often painful and quite often frustrating process of dedicated, focused, mindful practice.

A lot of people are credited with these words of wisdom, most notably a music professor named Percy C. Buck:

> ## "An amateur practices until he gets it right. A professional practices until he can't get it wrong!"

That's mastery in a nutshell.

Do genuine Masters get bored? Do they feel the pain? Do they get frustrated?

Of course they do—but when they get bored, they practice anyway.

When they feel the pain, they know they're getting stronger.

They know that frustration is the well from which all wisdom springs!

It's not complicated. Mastery is the product of hard work, focus and perseverance.

Dan Pink is right in emphasizing mastery as a key to motivation. Best of all, it's a self-perpetuating cycle.

Your enjoyment grows in direct proportion to your mastery. As your talents and skills expand, so do your opportunities—so does your sense of purpose.

MASTERING SELF

Before you can lead others in the pursuit of mastery, you've got to master your "self."

> ## "MASTERING OTHERS IS STRENGTH.
> ## MASTERING YOURSELF IS TRUE POWER."
>
> ~LAO TZU

An effective leader practices self-mastery. Not mastery for the purpose of command and control over others, but rather as the continual commitment to self-improvement, learning, growth and development.

If you want others to trust your leadership, respect your authority, and become partners in your vision, live as an example of genuine mastery.

More than any other quality of leadership, self-mastery is the one over which you have the most control.

You can't always control circumstances and conditions.

You most certainly can't always control people.

You can't control how people are going to react to your decisions and actions as a leader.

You can always learn and grow and perfect your talents, skills and abilities as a person—and as a leader.

Your commitment and willingness to improve becomes a powerful force that inspires others— your primary role as a leader.

Too many in leadership positions take a "do as I say and not as I do" approach to personal and professional development. This might work for 5 year-olds, but it carries no weight with your employees or the people you serve.

If you expect others to improve—improve yourself.

As with everything we're talking about, be a living example for the behavior and performance you expect from others.

As you improve, you inspire improvement in others. This extends also to the concept of "partner leadership" where you openly solicit constructive feedback from others, including subordinates.

If you expect others to improve, don't just tell them what they need to change, ask them for their input on how *you* can improve, too.

In *Carrots and Sticks Don't Work,* Paul Marciano talks about the power in this concept of a productive partnership between leaders and followers:

> Partners continually provide one another with ongoing supportive feedback. They do so out of respect for one another and because of their interest in achieving common goals. Thus, partners become each other's best coaches and push one another to excel. When one partner improves, the overall skill level of the partnership increases.

The problem with carrots and sticks is that people aren't donkeys!

People have a natural tendency toward collaboration. They'd rather be partners than beasts of burden, no matter what the potential rewards. This strategy helps you exploit the full potential of the "student to student" relationship we discussed earlier—an example of true partnership.

Once again you see the capacity of sharing to increase performance. As each individual, up and down the line, shares feedback that contributes to individual improvement, the team and the organization improves, often exponentially.

Jim Yong Kim, president of the World Bank said:

> No matter how good you think you are as a leader, my goodness, the people around you will have all kinds of ideas for how you can get better. So for me, the most fundamental thing about leadership is to have the humility to continue to get feedback and to try to get better—because your job is to try to help everybody else get better.

For this dynamic to work successfully, everyone, including those at the top, must be committed to continual self-improvement.

It may seem I'm obsessed to a degree with "self" improvement.

Some people challenge me on that point. They'll say that too much emphasis on self-improvement is, well—selfish.

I say that self-improvement is the least selfish thing you can do for others.

As you improve yourself, you become more valuable to others. You become a greater resource to your team, your organization and your community.

When everyone in an organization is committed to self-improvement—to personal and professional mastery—the entire organization becomes stronger, better, more productive, innovative and progressive.

At the risk of beating the dead horse even more, even a small improvement in each individual produces an exponential return.

I remember a story I once heard about a basketball coach who was trying to improve a struggling team. One of his first observations is that they were, as a team, lousy free-throw shooters.

Many coaches in this case would focus either on the top shooters and try to get more production there, or would commit a large effort to improving the weakest shooters. Instead, this coach set a goal. Every individual player would improve *just one percent.*

Together, the gains of just one percent for each individual far exceeded what could reasonably be expected by trying to extract bigger gains from just a few players.

It worked.

With each player contributing something, the overall performance of the team skyrocketed.

When each individual commits to the concept of personal mastery and continual self-improvement, the team and the organization become much more powerful.

EVEN THE SENSEI NEEDS A SENSEI

If you want to lead and inspire others, start with you. This is one area in leadership where it's essential to provide an example from the top down.

A genuine Master is always seeking out a new teacher. Sadly, many leaders stop looking for their next Master.

Here's a mind boggling revelation I found in an article by Nancy Zentis from the Institute of Organization Development blog:

> A recent study of 200 companies conducted by Stanford University found: Nearly 66% of CEOs do not receive coaching or leadership advice from outside consultants or coaches, while 100% of them stated that they are receptive to making changes based on feedback ...
>
> ... Lonely at the top resonates for most CEOs.

In regard to coaching and development, what do business leaders need and want?

> Many CEOs identified the need for coaching to improve

these competencies: sharing leadership, delegation, conflict management, team building, and mentoring.

These desirable competencies are exactly the traditional characteristics of the Sensei.

The Sensei not only trains his own martial skills, but he also continually works to improve as a teacher, mentor and coach.

An authentic Master embraces this process. It's all about continual learning, growth and development, no matter how high you are in rank, authority or responsibility.

This part of the article really bothered me:

At the bottom were softer skills such as: motivation, compassion/empathy, and persuasion.

At the bottom?

You don't lead process—you don't lead systems or equipment.

You lead people!

And people require compassion, empathy and sometimes even persuasion!

Don't ignore the power of these so called "soft" skills. Your ability to motivate, express compassion, inspire, encourage, and persuade are your most powerful assets as a leader.

JIM BOUCHARD

PERSONAL DEVELOPMENT AND PROFESSIONAL PERFORMANCE ARE INSEPARABLE

An article from *Harvard Business Review,* "Making Business Personal," highlights two remarkable companies that embrace this principle:

> These companies operate on the foundational assumptions that adults can grow; that not only is attention to the bottom line and the personal growth of all employees desirable, but the two are interdependent; that both profitability and individual development rely on structures that are built into every aspect of how the company operates; and that people grow through the proper combination of challenge and support, which includes recognizing and transcending their blind spots, limitations, and internal resistance to change.

It's time for more organizations to get on board.

Over the years I've had countless people tell me that their practice of martial arts, or their understanding of the philosophy, has opened new levels of performance and achievement.

Why?

It's certainly not the kicking and punching. You can achieve the same results in any challenging, meaningful, worthwhile pursuit.

It's the combination of "challenge and support" emphasized in the *HBR* piece. People grow in direct response to challenge. Ability, skill, talent as well as confidence and competency all grow in direct proportion to the level of challenge you face and opportunities available to test yourself under pressure.

People grow through the martial arts experience because it is challenging and because they develop with the support and encouragement of the Sensei and their peers.

You want people to grow? Be a supportive, nourishing leader. Develop a culture that encourages and supports development and rewards learning, growth and development at all levels.

The *HBR* article continues …

> Every job should be like a towrope, so that as you grab hold of the job, the very process of doing the work pulls you up the mountain.

Cultivate an environment where people enthusiastically embrace new challenges. Be a model of that enthusiasm. The mettle of a warrior is only tested in battle—you need challenges to discover and develop the highest levels of performance.

If you want to lead warriors—be a warrior.

IF YOU WANT TO LEAD MASTERY, BE THE MASTER

As I keep saying, a true Master is never finished and never satisfied. Keep that ideal of Beginner's Mind we talked about earlier and embed that mindset in your organization.

The process of mastery demands:

CONSTANT INTROSPECTION

A WILLINGNESS TO BE OPEN TO SINCERE AND PRODUCTIVE CRITICISM

AN ENTHUSIASM FOR ACCEPTING NEW CHALLENGES AND OPPORTUNITIES FOR GROWTH

THE COURAGE TO RISK FAILURES IN PURSUIT OF GREATER ACHIEVEMENT

Embed the mindset of Mastery throughout your organization's culture.

Cultivate your own mastery, and support each individual in your organization in their pursuit of mastery—from leadership to the front lines.

"I FEAR NOT THE MAN WHO HAS PRACTICED 10,000 KICKS ONCE, BUT I FEAR THE MAN WHO HAS PRACTICED ONE KICK 10,000 TIMES."

~BRUCE LEE

4. BE CONFIDENT, BE HUMBLE, AND LEAD BY EXAMPLE

Be courageous yet sensitive, authoritative without being authoritarian.

> "WHEN THE PEOPLE ARE NOT IN AWE OF YOUR MAJESTY THEN GREAT MAJESTY HAS BEEN ACHIEVED."
>
> ~LAO TZU

Confidence is, of course, an attractive quality for a leader. People do tend to follow leaders who possess a healthy level of confidence, but only when that confidence is built on a solid foundation of trust and credibility.

They want to know you are someone who is willing to walk the walk with them—that you are someone willing to lead by example.

Confidence is one of the most poorly understood characteristics of human behavior, and that makes it hard to get a grip on it.

As I said earlier—most people equate confidence with certainty. To a point that's true, but confidence is more about certainty in your *ability* to perform adequately, or even to your best, in the present situation.

Executive strategist Eric Douglas posted a commentary on *LinkedIn*. Citing a study on the relationship between confidence and certainty, he found:

> Leaders who were confident but relatively uncertain were viewed as more effective, more likely to foster creative thinking and independent thinking. Those who were confident and certain were viewed as authoritarian and inflexible.

How can confidence and uncertainty be the right combination for an effective leader?

How can uncertainty and confidence even fit together in the same head space?

Remember from our discussion on courage—and this is critical if you want to be an effective leader ...

... confidence is NOT surety in an outcome! It's certainty in your ability to perform!

The dictionary definition of confidence most useful to this discussion is:

> Belief in oneself and one's powers or abilities; self-confidence; self-reliance; assurance

During my research I studied several definitions of confidence. I didn't find *one* mention of outcome or result—not a single reference. So what do you call it when a fighter calls the round for a knockout or a football player guarantees victory? Isn't *that* confidence?

Not always. Not even usually. Most of the time, that's just plain arrogance.

A cocky, chest thumping display of confidence may just be a mask. That mask of arrogance often hides deep rooted insecurity, a complete lack of self-assurance.

True confidence attracts willing followers.

Arrogance repels them.

True confidence is expressed more subtly—through what we call, *"humility."*

Humility is a quiet expression of reserve. You might not know with certainty that you're going to win the fight, but you damn sure know you deserve to be in the ring.

Tempered by humility, your confidence is independent of the desired or expected outcome.

Humility is the quality that keeps your mind and heart open to input from other people, even from the people who work for you.

Abraham Lincoln was renowned for his self-effacing and humble demeanor. In *Lincoln on Leadership,* Donald T. Phillips writes:

> Lincoln essentially treated his subordinates as equals;
> they were colleagues in a joint effort. He had enough

> confidence in himself that he was not threatened by skillful generals or able cabinet officials. Rather than surround himself with 'yes' men, he associated with people who really knew their business, people from whom he could learn something ...

Note the emphasis on confidence. Genuine humility is not possible without true confidence.

With humility, true confidence appears to others as a quiet reserve that shows that while you believe in your ability to perform effectively in any given moment, you are not arrogant or cocksure.

Humility also makes it possible for you to be a good follower yourself, and the best leaders are always good followers.

Robert E. Kelley, author of *The Power of Followership,* wrote:

> Followership is not a person, but a role, and what distinguishes followers from leaders is not intelligence or character, but the role they play.

Kelley also said:

> Instead of seeing the leadership role as superior to and more effective than the role of the follower, we can think of them as equal but different activities.

More evidence that the partnership between leader and follower is far more powerful than the autocratic leader shouting orders from the rear while mounted on his high horse.

You inspire followers by your willingness to be a good follower yourself. You can only operate effectively in both roles when you have the confidence to realize that following does not diminish your status as a leader and when you have the humility to embrace the role of follower with the same enthusiasm as you bring to your role as leader.

This is the type of confidence that makes a leader attractive—whether that leader is in a position of authority or command, or standing shoulder to shoulder with you in the trenches.

This is the type of confidence that will make you an effective person and an effective leader at any level, whether you want to work in command and control or on the front lines.

Master Jhoon Rhee is a pioneer in contemporary martial arts and to my mind one of the world's greatest living philosophers.

Master Rhee developed a Student Creed for his own students and generously shared his creed with martial artists all over the world. After I met Master Rhee, I started a daily practice of sharing his creed with my students.

His creed begins with this affirmation:

To build true confidence, through knowledge in the mind, honesty in the heart, and strength in the body.

This isn't about a guaranteed result. It's about training!

Master Rhee specifies the areas where you have control of developing authentic self-confidence, through your sincere commitment to learning, honesty and personal development in mind, body and spirit.

You cannot guarantee an outcome, but you can train. You

can guarantee that you're prepared to give your best when you're called to face your toughest challenges.

WALK THE WALK

I keep beating this drum, but if there is one thing you can do as a leader to inspire the highest levels of performance in others, it's to lead by example.

Long ago the master military strategist Sun Tzu said:

"A LEADER LEADS BY EXAMPLE, NOT BY FORCE."

With the benefit of experience and after having made plenty of mistakes along the way, I found this truth:

PEOPLE FOLLOW EXAMPLES MUCH MORE ENTHUSIASTICALLY THAN THEY DO ORDERS.

If you want to lead effectively—model the behavior you expect from others.

If you say you're going to do something—do it.

If you're wrong and you know it, own it.

Say what you mean—and mean what you say.

These days words come back to haunt you like never before. Social media, email and camera phones have changed the way our words are captured. Once you open your mouth, there's no taking it back.

Don't lie, don't cover up, don't abdicate responsibility or shift the blame to others. People understand mistakes. They have no respect for liars and fakers.

Above all, your character—how you act—determines whether or not people will trust and follow you.

Circumstances and conditions may be outside your control, but your demeanor under pressure provides the most revealing insight into your character.

Walking the walk means being willing to do what you expect others to do. There is no better way to establish credibility with your followers than to be willing to pick up a shovel when a ditch needs to be dug—instead of just ordering others to jump in the hole.

Look—your Mama probably taught you this stuff when you were a kid.

Like everything else we're talking about, you've got to practice—not only what you preach, but what you do.

If you're going to talk the talk—you'd better walk the walk!

5. BE FLEXIBLE, ADAPTABLE AND COMFORTABLE WITH UNCERTAINTY

Be prepared for every possibility and contingency. Be receptive to the rapid flow of new information and rapidly changing conditions. Be willing to act quickly to exploit new opportunities. Learn from the past but embrace the power of change.

In *Principle Centered Leadership,* renowned author Stephen R. Covey shares a profile of the leader who embraces change:

> They're not slavishly chained to their plans and schedules. They don't condemn themselves for every foolish mistake or social blunder. They don't brood about yesterday or daydream about tomorrow. They live sensibly in the present, carefully plan the future, and flexibly adapt to changing circumstances.

That's the perfect description of The Sensei Leader.

Honor tradition and be a good steward of immutable values and principles from the past. At the same time, approach each new day with an open mind, ready to embrace the opportunities that come with change and commit yourself to exploration, creativity and innovation—the life blood of human progress.

Tradition is important, but it's equally important not to let vestigial traditions stand in the way of meaningful progress.

I found a post by Dan Rockwell, author of the *Leadership-Freak* blog titled: "Three Qualities Traditional Leaders Reject."

Rockwell writes:

> Traditional leaders are unwelcoming. Traditional leaders expect you to receive their ideas; they don't receive yours.

Are you freaking kidding me?

Those leaders are obviously following the WRONG tradition!!!

I was about ready to lose my traditional mind!

I was ready to come out with sword drawn ready to defend the sacred honor of the traditional leaders I admire!

Thankfully, I took a deep breath and continued reading the rest of Rockwell's article:

> Stop looking down your nose at outsiders, front line employees, and new hires.
>
> Adapt to them; don't force them to adapt to you.

TRADITION SHOULD INFORM PROGRESS, NOT RESTRICT IT

I once asked Master Yang about a struggle I was having in separating effective techniques from those that seemed to be taught by rote, just because they had always been taught.

He told me, "Jim, just because it's old—*doesn't make it right!*"

Perhaps more than ever before, today's leader must be flexible not just in response to changing conditions but, more importantly, in response to people. Even the smallest organizations are now part a diverse cultural and environmental paradigm that previous generations could have never imagined.

One of the most difficult and persistent challenges in business leadership today is that of generational diversity. Generation X, Generation Y, Millennials—you can't tell the players without a scorecard!

Stop dealing with *people,* and start dealing with the *person.* An organization is a collection of individuals, and each individual has a unique set of values, needs, desires and ambitions.

These days, we're hopelessly addicted to group assessments, statistics, labels, trends, and generalizations. Today's leader has to be responsive to the individual as well as the group.

The behavior of the group is only typical, not specific.

Any particular individual may behave radically different

171

than the norm identified by a group assessment. Don't get me wrong, research is important and it's helpful to identify trends. It's just not productive to treat any one person as strictly part of demographic group.

It's difficult to set aside generalizations. As much as I know better, I'm guilty of judging the person by the group from time to time.

Throughout my martial arts career, I've been vocal and somewhat intractable about my belief that kids today are lazier, harder to motivate and more difficult to teach than those of a few years ago—and there's plenty of research that supports that position!

For the first time since these things have been measured, studies show a marked decline in conceptual thinking and problem solving abilities in kids in grades K through 12. Obesity and associated health issues in this same age are at an all-time high—and trending north.

Does that mean that all kids are becoming stupid, fat and lazy?

Of course not.

An effective leader does not judge or treat any particular individual based on the behavior or dynamic of the group. There are always notable individual exceptions.

Whenever I catch myself lapsing into generalization, I think about Marcus …

Marcus was a student in my martial arts program. At the time he was about 8, he was preparing for his blue belt, one of our intermediate ranks. This test would be special because it was his last test with us. His Dad was a Navy Chief, and they were about to be transferred to a base in Florida.

Before the test, Marcus's Mom came to me and said Marcus had all the material he needed for his green belt. Believe me, this was not the first time a proud and doting mom had approached me angling for a double promotion or special consideration for her talented child.

My face must have betrayed my annoyance because she quickly added, "I don't expect him to jump a rank—it's just that he's been working very hard on the extra material. He really loves you and it would mean a lot to him if he could show it to you before we leave."

Turning down such a sincere and sentimental request would certainly conflict with my commitment to compassionate leadership, wouldn't it?

Frankly, what was the harm? If Marcus wanted to show off his material, he'd earned the right. Maybe he'd be a good example for some of the others.

Long story short—Marcus didn't just have the material— he nailed it!

He wasn't as good as the kids who were going for their green belts—he was better than any of them—*way better.*

I was very pleased with Marcus, but at the same time I wanted to know how he got all the extra material. I discourage instructors from advancing students too fast. Pushing material can prevent a student from really absorbing the material on a deep enough level and in some cases, pushing a student too fast can be discouraging and frustrating.

I asked Mom to tell me who gave Marcus all the extra material.

"Nobody," she said, "he did it himself!"

It turns out Marcus had asked his mother to stay after classes so he could watch the more advanced kids. He'd learn a technique or two, then go home and practice. When he thought he had it, he'd beg mom to stay again, and so on.

"Who taught him how to do this?" I asked mom.

"Nobody," she repeated, "he did it all by himself."

Marcus was definitely an exception to the rule. You better believe he left that day with a green belt.

The problem with statistics, trends and generalizations is that while they hold some truth reflective of the performance of a group, you've got to look past the metrics to identify the exceptions—and the exceptional.

If you're going to maximize engagement and performance, you've got to look deeper than the statistics and treat people as individuals.

Today, for example, many studies and polls indicate that Millennials are more engaged by a sense of purpose than by money, but it's a mistake to ignore the outliers who are more motivated by financial rewards.

Surveys also indicate that women with children in your organization tend to value flex time more than other benefits, but some significant exceptions prefer the opportunity for advancement. These women trend more with male demographics—they want increased responsibility and more opportunities to focus on career and job.

Finally, remember that even your best employees are still wired to put their own needs and interests above yours–*and there's nothing wrong with that!*

You're the leader. You're the steward of the vision.

It's up to you as a leader to inspire others to buy in to your overarching goals and objectives.

The strongest engagement occurs when you're able to align organizational vision and objectives with the needs and desires of your people, and you can only do that by understanding each individual—and by being flexible and responsive to those needs and desires.

You can't be all things to all employees, but understanding the individual gives you the ability to determine how best to increase engagement and performance.

You have little chance of satisfying everyone, especially your top performers, by myopically reacting to group trends.

Sometimes your best people are the exceptions— like Marcus!

THE UNCERTAINTY CONUNDRUM

I talked earlier about embracing uncertainty as a means to developing confidence and courage. Many experts today see the ability to manage uncertainty as an important marker to determine your capacity for leadership.

In their article, "Acceptance of Uncertainty as an Indicator of Effective Leadership," Randall White and Sandra Shullman of Executive Development Group highlight the importance of a leader's ability to handle uncertainty:

> ... we suggest that being an effective leader is contingent on the ability to deal with ambiguity and its resulting cognitive-affective reaction, uncertainty. Those who can keep the experience of uncertainty to a tolerable level can keep more options open and embrace ambiguity as an opportunity to bring people and options together to learn and adapt collectively as they find their way.

This is no surprise to The Sensei Leader. The warrior is only truly tested in battle, and as General Patton said, "Battle is an orgy of disorder."

Patton also said:

"PREPARE FOR THE UNKNOWN BY STUDYING HOW OTHERS IN THE PAST HAVE COPED WITH THE UNFORESEEABLE AND THE UNPREDICTABLE."

The best leaders accept uncertainty, just as they accept fear.

They understand that uncertainty presents an opportunity to test one's ingenuity, creativity and adaptability under pressure.

Condition yourself to deal with the unexpected, with uncertainty, fear and even chaos.

The more comfortable and confident you are under those conditions, the more effective your performance as a leader.

"UNCERTAINTY IS NOT AN INDICATION OF POOR LEADERSHIP; IT UNDERSCORES THE NEED FOR LEADERSHIP."

~ANDY STANLEY

6. BE A SKILLED COMMUNICATOR

Communicate sincerely, honestly, and transparently.

From a report by Chad Brooks on *FOXBusiness.com:*

> While they may be charged with leading their companies, business executives still have plenty of room for improvement when it comes to their leadership skills, a new study finds.

> Research from communications firm Ketchum revealed that just 34 percent of consumers worldwide view business chiefs as effective leaders and only 35 percent believe they are effective communicators.

The most effective leaders are effective communicators.

Who you are as a leader becomes reality in the minds and hearts of others through what you say, how you say it, and most importantly, how people hear you.

I keep singing this song, but a leader is someone with the ability to attract willing followers. Trust plays a big part in that ability and the key to trust is effective, clear communication consistent with your values and actions.

Granted, it's not always easy to preserve this trust, especially when tough decisions have to be made. And it's not always fair or accurate to accuse the leader of a lack of compassion, authenticity, or competence when you have to make those tough decisions.

Communication is a key expression of caring and compassion. If you care, and you want people to know you care, you've got to let them know. If you want to earn their trust, they've got to know you're listening to their needs, concerns, and desires.

Effective communication is not just what you say. It's also what you hear and who you're willing to listen to. Effective communication flows two ways. The most effective leader is a finely tuned receiver as well as a powerful transmitter.

Support and encourage open and honest communication from the bottom up as well as the top down. Put systems in place to facilitate an unimpeded flow of information between levels.

Most of all, demonstrate by example that you are willing to listen—willing to hear what people have to say. Listen with your heart and mind as well as your ears.

Back to the report:

> "In 2012, we found that leadership credibility hinged on a combination of open and transparent communication, decisive action and the personal presence of the leader," said Rod Cartwright, partner and director of Ketchum's Global Corporate Practice. "With the crisis of leadership and communication continuing to have a direct commercial impact, our 2013 study shows

that this formula for establishing meaningful, authentic leadership remains as robust as ever and will only grow in importance over the coming decade."

The trust of followers, consumers, employees and peers is earned. That trust is dependent on your ability to truly listen and your ability to communicate with clarity, meaning and sincerity.

WHAT YOU SHOULD BE TALKING ABOUT

Conventional wisdom emphasizes "vision" as one of the most important messages a leader must communicate. Simon Sinek observes:

> There is an inextricable link between leadership and communication. Leaders are the ones who can clearly communicate their vision...

> Great leaders don't spend all their time talking about what they can do. Great leaders talk about what they can see.

Vision is important and inspiring, but don't leave it there. Drill deeper.

What is it about your vision that inspires the individual?

Great leaders communicate effectively in three major areas

that inspire individual performance and unite people in a common cause:

PURPOSE

MEANING

RECOGNITION

Effective leaders are also good at delivering bad news and criticism. This part of the job is tough, but any hesitancy or inability on your part to communicate the bad along with the good smacks of cowardice or deception.

Let's start with the good stuff ...

PURPOSE & MEANING

You must communicate a clear sense of purpose and meaning, both for the organization and for the individual.

You don't have to be the stereotypical "motivational speaker" to inspire and communicate a clear sense of purpose.

You don't have to be loud—you have to be committed. You have to be sincere, enthusiastic, and consistent ...

"INSPIRATIONAL LEADERS NEED TO HAVE
A WINNING MENTALITY IN ORDER TO
INSPIRE RESPECT. IT IS HARD TO TRUST
IN THE LEADERSHIP OF SOMEONE WHO
IS HALF-HEARTED ABOUT THEIR
PURPOSE, OR ONLY SPORADIC IN
FOCUS OR ENTHUSIASM."

~SEBASTIAN COE

One of the most powerful forces driving human performance is the need for meaning and purpose and the desire to be recognized for one's contribution. To feel successful, fulfilled and happy, people need to know that they are contributing real value to others.

If you want to engage individuals in the mission of the group, you've got to communicate a clear sense of meaning and purpose. They've got to own the mission.

The words you choose have a tremendous impact on engagement:

It's not my purpose—it's OUR purpose. It's not what it means to me—it's what it means to US.

You don't motivate people by command and control—you inspire them by sharing a meaningful purpose.

THE POWER OF RECOGNITION

Sam Walton said:

"WE LET FOLKS KNOW WE'RE INTERESTED IN THEM AND THAT THEY'RE VITAL TO US. 'CAUSE THEY ARE."

It's that simple.

Recognition is an extremely powerful force for inspiring others. I lost sight of this power at one point and seriously considered eliminating ranks at my martial arts center.

I thought eliminating the ranks would serve two purposes:

First—I was frustrated with students and parents who valued rank over practice. I was afraid that the real process of perfecting the art and perfecting the self was somehow getting lost, replaced by "the belt chase."

The pretty colored belts, along with the associated pomp and ceremony, and the bragging rights, seemed to be more important to some students than becoming a stronger martial artist and a stronger person.

Next—I'd become completely intoxicated with the idea that, at some point, a martial artist shouldn't need the recognition that comes with rank. I thought that the learning and the practice itself should be more important than a belt or a trophy.

Around this time I was exploring, for myself, the more esoteric levels of ego diminishment so many people associate with martial arts. I thought the joy of development should be its own reward—and I thought anyone else who practiced the arts sincerely would *(and should)* feel the same way.

I had forgotten how important the recognition of rank had been to me.

I forgot how earning that belt had confirmed, in my mind, my transformation from a self-destructive loser to a Sensei.

I dropped out of college twice before I found the discipline necessary to earn my Black Belt. Earning my rank marked the first time in my life I'd completed any significant or worthwhile endeavor.

My Black Belt promotion was also the first time I was recognized in a formal way for doing anything meaningful. Privately, it was my first tangible acknowledgment that I was no longer a drug addict, dropout, or loser—now I was a Black Belt.

How could I have lost sight of what this recognition meant to me?

Worse—how could I not see how important those ranks were to my students?

I was ready to rob them of the same experience that literally changed my life!

Fortunately, I had the sense to seek out some other opinions before I imposed this sweeping reform.

Peter Storey was a federal judge.

I was certainly impressed by his position, and he had almost instantly earned my respect and admiration.

There is still a huge part of me that regrets how much time I've wasted in my life and how many opportunities I've squandered. I admit openly that I am impressed by successful people who apply themselves to better ends than I did.

Peter also became an instant friend. I saw a deep, understanding nature in him, and he seemed to me to be a sincere human being as well as a genuine leader.

Peter had just earned his yellow belt—the first earned rank in our system. I brought up the idea of dropping the ranks and asked him for his opinion.

All he said was, "Don't do it!"

He was adamant. "Absolutely not. That would be a huge mistake."

Peter explained that he could go ten years in his job without anyone giving him a pat on the back, thanking him for his efforts, or recognizing him for a job well-done.

On most days, the decisions he had to make pissed people off. Nobody likes to be sent to prison—and nobody is going to thank the judge who sent him there.

I'd never thought of it quite that way, but he certainly had my attention.

He talked about how much this rank meant to him and how much he appreciated the serious and thoughtful nature of our promotion ceremony, something I was very proud of.

As he talked, I remembered how much the yellow belt had meant to me.

To me, earning the yellow belt was the first time anyone

recognized me for any accomplishment, however small, since I started to turn my life around. It was still a long way from Black Belt, but it was a start—and someone had taken the time to acknowledge my work and give me a genuine pat on the back.

The recognition of someone you admire and trust is a powerful transformational force.

It serves as validation, an acknowledgment that your efforts mean something to others and that you're part of something larger than yourself.

To Peter and the other martial artists at Northern Chi, it also meant a connection to the long heritage of martial artists that had gone before them. It meant acceptance into a community, a fraternity of people dedicated to exploring their full potential.

Peter was right. I was wrong.

I kept the ranks. In fact, I placed an even greater emphasis on them.

If the ranks had lost some of their true purpose, that was my fault. It was up to me to make sure every student knew what those ranks really meant.

It is your obligation as a leader to recognize the work of others.

Zig Ziglar said, "Research indicates that employees have three prime needs: Interesting work, recognition for doing a good job, and being let in on things that are going on in the company."

Of the three, recognition may just be the most direct and

most impactful. The respected *McKinsey Quarterly* conducted a survey to find out what employees considered most important to their level of motivation.

> The respondents view three non-cash motivators—praise from immediate managers, leadership attention (for example, one-on-one conversations), and a chance to lead projects or task forces—as no less or even more effective motivators than the three highest-rated financial incentives: cash bonuses, increased base pay, and stock or stock options. The survey's top three non-financial motivators play critical roles in making employees feel that their companies value them, take their well-being seriously, and strive to create opportunities for career growth.

Recognition, praise, and the attention of a supervisor consistently rank among the top factors in employee engagement and motivation.

The Sensei Leader makes sure people know that their efforts are appreciated and acknowledges every meaningful step along the way.

CRITICISM

It's always inspiring, and let's admit it, it's fun to recognize people for good work.

There is nothing I enjoy more than promoting other martial artists to Black Belt. For me, that's payday. Seeing other people accomplish their rank validates my work—but first, we've got to get them there.

As important as recognition is your ability to offer honest, clear, and productive criticism.

Over 20 years of teaching martial arts, I've developed a technique for criticism that works in all but the most extreme cases. This technique works as well in the office as it does in the dojo.

Here's the trick:

First—find something to praise—and make sure it's real.

The youngest student can see through false praise.

The best teacher can always find some genuine achievement, no matter how small, on which to offer sincere praise and begin the process of building the student's confidence and expectations of improvement.

Using an example from the dojo—many martial artists practice long sets of choreographed movements. Systems borrowing the Japanese traditions call these exercises, *"kata."* Kata are often difficult to learn and require a great deal of concentration and practice.

You can say that kata is an exercise in perfection.

Of course keep in mind that "perfection is not a destination …" No matter how hard you work, there will be something that needs improving.

In the early stages of learning a kata, it's quite normal for an instructor to find few, if any, redeeming qualities in that student's performance.

Frankly, the form, or kata, can look like a complete mess!

You're faced with a choice. You can barrage the student with corrections—or you can find one thing the student did well and start there.

Don't get me wrong. Correction is important. In this era of getting a trophy for showing up, it's even more important that we train people, especially young people, to accept correction and criticism with the spirit of improvement.

Having said that—your correction will be far more effective if you can find one point where the student performs well, or an area where you've seen the student make some improvement.

People are more receptive to praise than criticism. A sincere word of encouragement or recognition opens the mind and the heart to the correction that will follow.

Make your encouragement specific, never general.

"That looks pretty good" is meaningless. It's hollow.

Insincere praise only means you're not paying attention or you don't really care—especially when the student knows he's not up to par.

In this example, I might say, "Your stances are much deeper

than they were last time I saw your form. That shows some real improvement."

Now that I've established a positive foundation, I can add a positive correction—with emphasis on the positive:

"Now that you have a stronger stance, let's look at what you're doing with your hips and see if we can draw more power from your stance and get it to your strikes."

Positive criticism is usually much more effective than negative criticism. People respond better emotionally to positive direction, but it's also much more efficient. You can usually replace a dozen "don'ts" with one "do."

When you focus on the negative, you're creating a list of filtered actions that someone has to recall in order to avoid repeating the mistake or the incorrect behavior. That list can be quite long.

When you focus on the positive, you reinforce the desired action—in one step.

Over thirty years of teaching and leadership, this method has defined my teaching and leadership style.

By focusing on positive correction, I've earned the trust of many students who came to me from other, more authoritative instructors because, under those instructors, they were making little or no progress.

Sometimes criticism must be direct and unfiltered—even harsh. Those times mark exceptions, not the rule.

If you hear yourself sounding like the bad-ass drill sergeant too often—it's time to look in the mirror.

Most of the time you can find something positive and build

from there. Sincere praise and meaningful recognition build the foundation for exceptional performance.

YOU WANT THE GOOD NEWS FIRST, OR THE BAD NEWS?

Should you let people know when you're worried? Should you tell people when the organization is in trouble?

Well, there's not always an easy answer, but in most situations—yes!

It's human nature to want to share the pain to a degree. It is lonely at the top, and when you have no one else to turn to, it's natural to turn to those closest to you, even if they work for you.

Be very careful when you're venting or blowing off steam. You don't want people to see you crying in your beer. Transparency isn't about dumping your problems on someone else, especially your followers.

On the other hand, there's nothing that breeds mistrust faster than the appearance that you're hiding something important—even if your sincere intention is to protect people from bad news.

The challenge is to share a problem or a challenge in such a way that you inspire a collective effort to find a solution.

The key is what Dov Baron calls "vulnerability." From his book, *Fiercely Loyal:*

> To be a great leader, you must become masterful at relationships by embracing vulnerability and finding a way to bring vulnerability and courage together, not only in yourself, but also in all those who surrounded you. Such an act requires real intimacy—and there is no real or lasting intimacy without raw, honest vulnerability.

Put yourself in their shoes.

It may be very important for them to know that there is a downturn in sales, a problem with production or that the company is suffering the effects of outside economic conditions. You may tell everyone that you're going to go without your salary to help the company weather the storm.

To someone on the front lines, your announcement might show them they've got a leader they can count on. It might also mean they'd better start looking for another job!

It's important to be as transparent as possible, but you don't lessen your burden by scaring others, and your objective shouldn't be to shock people into action.

Your goal is to solicit the support of your team so you can all work together to find a solution …

… Focus on the solution!

Be straightforward and clinical about the challenges you face. Present the facts without adding drama.

Be sure everyone understands clearly the present situation, and make sure they know that you understand and appreciate the impact of the situation on each of them as individuals.

Then — ask.

Ask for ideas.

Draw on the experience, wisdom
and dedication of your team.

Ask them to develop solutions
based on individual expertise
and experience.

What can each person do to
contribute to moving
the organization forward?

Most of all, assure your people that you're dedicated to success. You're not sharing a difficult situation because you're ready to fold the tents—if that's the case, fold 'em!

Appeal for a dedicated team effort because you know that together, you can solve the problem and build a stronger, more resilient and successful organization.

DON'T BE AN "UNDERCOVER BOSS!"

Remember that in terms of sheer volume, most of the practical knowledge and intellectual capital in any organization exists in the ranks, not in the highest positions.

Most important information about current conditions originates on the front lines, too— those people are on the point. They're your connection to the entire organization and to the outside world.

This is one of the many reasons it's important to become a skilled and receptive listener.

You've also got to cultivate a process that facilitates the clear and timely flow of information back and forth through all levels. To do this, you've got to encourage leaders at all levels and support those people who are willing to communicate openly and honestly.

"Do you like the TV show, Undercover Boss?"

I ask that question nearly every time I do a Sensei Leader presentation. At this point, most of the people in the room start sharing anecdotes from their favorite episodes—it seems most business folks love the show.

"I hate it!"

When I say that, the room usually goes dead silent.

How can I hate such an entertaining and informative program? It has nothing to do with the quality of the show and I admit I do get sucked into it from time to time, but still—it drives me up a wall—*why?*

Because I can't understand how the hell so many top CEOs are so surprised to learn about how their people feel on the front lines!

They shouldn't be!

Their ignorance is inevitably a direct result of a lack of two-way communication.

In the spirit of full disclosure, I've always been a micro-business guy. I've never run a huge corporation. I've never had more than a couple of employees at a time.

Like most small business operators, I work shoulder to shoulder with everyone in my organization. I can't help but see and hear most everything, even things they'd probably rather I didn't! How can I possibly expect the CEO of a large organization of a thousand or more people to sit down and engage every single employee in the organization on that same level?

I don't.

I do suggest you engage some of them on regular basis—if you want them to be engaged in your mission.

Sam Walton built the largest retail empire on earth by engaging all of his employees on a very personal level.

While he was still running the company, he mandated that everyone in management spend time each year on the front lines. This remarkable policy put top executives and managers shoulder to shoulder with the people on the front lines. He put managers and executives in positions where they would experience life in the trenches first hand and, even more important, where they could hear the voices of the people on the ground who really make the company work.

I realize that if you're the CEO of an organization with

10,000 employees, it's just impossible to sit down with each and every one of them individually, but here's what you can do …

> YOU CAN DEDICATE TIME TO SPEND WITH A FEW OF THEM ON A REGULAR BASIS.

> YOU CAN BUILD A CULTURE OF SINCERE INTEREST.

> YOU CAN INSIST THAT SUPERVISORS SPEND TIME UNDERSTANDING THE NEEDS, DESIRES AND MOTIVATIONS OF THE PEOPLE DIRECTLY IN THEIR CARE.

Everyone should have direct access to their immediate supervisor. Supervisors should have their eyes, ears, hearts and minds open to the people who serve under them.

You don't need to disguise yourself on a reality show to connect with the troops.

HONESTY AND TRANSPARENCY

Carly Fiorina is a former CEO of Hewlett-Packard. As I write this, she is considered by many as a serious contender to be America's first woman president.

In an interview with FOX News, Fiorina spoke about the importance of transparency:

> ... leadership has to be transparent, because people need to know that they can count on their leaders— that they can count on their leader's character, that they can count on their leader's competence, that they can count on their leader's motivation. And you can't count on character, competence or motivation unless you can see what the leader is doing.

> And that's why transparency is so important and that's why a lack of transparency becomes corrosive over time, to trust.

Honesty and transparency must be practiced at all times.

Sadly, too many leaders today compromise this principle. They often pay a hefty price for breaking this rule, but even more sadly, they often burden their followers with an heavier toll.

Transparency is not always comfortable, and honesty is not always easy. In the moment, a frank and honest approach might ruffle feathers—even instigate an angry response.

In the long run, your ability to be frank and honest will earn you the respect of your followers. They may not like what you have to say in the moment, but over time they will appreciate your candor and they'll respond with loyalty, devotion and sometimes, if you're lucky—even sincere affection.

There has never been an American leader more respected and loved by his followers than General Robert E. Lee.

To this day, Lee's lessons on leadership are studied and emulated, here and around the world. One of his most distinguishing characteristics was his ability to connect on a very personal level with his troops. He was a master communicator revered for his sincerity and honesty.

General Lee left us this simple leadership rule:

"YOU MUST STUDY TO BE FRANK WITH THE WORLD: FRANKNESS IS THE CHILD OF HONESTY AND COURAGE. SAY JUST WHAT YOU MEAN TO DO ON EVERY OCCASION, AND TAKE IT FOR GRANTED THAT YOU MEAN TO DO RIGHT."

Be honest. Enough said.

7. Be a dedicated teacher, coach and mentor

Know when to encourage and when to correct. Bring out the best in others and confidently train others to surpass you in talent, skill and ability.

To me, this is the most important chapter in this book.

Great leaders are always effective teachers. I believe with all my heart that the only way to be a great leader is to teach and mentor others—to help them become leaders too.

Tom Peters wrote:

"Leaders don't create followers— they create more leaders."

You create leaders by being a dedicated teacher, coach, and mentor, by helping other people realize their true potential.

Is this a new paradigm in leadership?

Leadership experts and co-authors Charles Manz and Henry Sims seem to think so:

In many modern situations, the most appropriate leader is one who can lead others to lead themselves.

We call this powerful new kind of leadership, *Super-Leadership.*

I agree with their premise entirely; however, I dispute their claim that this is a new type of leadership!

About 2,500 years ago, Lao Tzu said:

"A LEADER IS BEST WHEN PEOPLE BARELY KNOW HE EXISTS. WHEN HIS WORK IS DONE, HIS AIM FULFILLED, THEY WILL SAY: WE DID IT OURSELVES."

The idea of expanding one's own effectiveness by empowering others is certainly not new, but it is an idea that merits a revival.

I'm sure Manz and Sims would acknowledge Lao Tzu's contribution to this philosophy—they use the exact quotation you just read in their article. They continue:

The SuperLeader's strength is greatly enhanced since it's drawn from the strength of many people who have been encouraged to grow, flourish and become important contributors. The SuperLeader becomes "Super" through the talents and capabilities of others. As self-leadership is nurtured, the power for progress is unleashed.

Manz and Sims may very well be black belts! Many of my Masters shared exactly that same philosophy.

As powerful and timely as these ideas are, many leaders are still reluctant to embrace the role of teacher and mentor. The Institute of Organization Development citing a Stanford University study reveals:

Another critical area of development for CEOs was "mentoring skills/developing internal talent ..."

Another critical area?

This may just be your most important role as a leader—mentoring, teaching and developing the skills of the people in your care.

In some traditions—in both martial arts and business, the Sensei or the executive can feel threatened by the ability and skill of a student or subordinate. In an overly authoritarian culture, the leader does not encourage development past his own skill level, but jealously guards his power and maintains authority by force.

What happens to the people under him?

These days—they quit. They move on to better opportunities for growth and development.

The best Sensei measures his success by the student that surpasses his own skills, talents and abilities. You can substitute the words follower, employee or subordinate— the aim is to develop people you serve to their full potential.

In this transformational culture, there is always room for

growth and development. Instead of feeling threatened, the leader looks for new ways to utilize the expanding skills and talents of everyone in his care. Innovation, initiative and creativity are recognized, nourished and rewarded.

When the Sensei or leader plays an active role in mentoring and training someone to exceed his skills, there is no threat. There is respect.

"THE MASTER EXCELS NOT BY TEACHING HIS STUDENTS TO EQUAL HIS ABILITIES;

THE MASTER EXCELS WHEN HIS STUDENT'S ABILITIES EXCEED HIS OWN."

~ANON.

I've trained many people who have become far better martial artists than I'll ever be. That's not a threat—*that's my job!*

Those people don't leave or reject me—they become loyal advocates and look to me to help them further develop.

They also become a great resource in my life and my organization. These are the people who afford me the time to develop other skills, talents and abilities as they assume some of my former roles and duties.

A few years ago I noticed something very interesting was happening around me. I didn't ask for this—it just started happening …

Before my students became Black Belts, they addressed me as Sensei.

The relationship still had the dynamic of teacher to student I talked about earlier and as students, they still felt some sense of dependence and deference toward me.

When I promoted my first Black Belts, and then later as I acknowledged some of these students with higher ranks and recognized them for equaling or even surpassing my skills and abilities in some way—those students started addressing me as *"Master."*

As I promote the student, the student elevates me.

As the student excels, my role shifts from simply teaching technique to mentoring and coaching that student to even higher levels of performance.

That's how you cultivate a powerful organization.

TEACH WITH QUESTIONS

Did you notice throughout this book that I ask a lot of questions? In a live presentation I ask even more.

Why?

Because nothing engages the mind as powerfully as a question. Questions, challenges and tests engage the learner in the process of thinking and problem solving.

Don't you learn more when you're part of an experience rather than just a passive recipient of information?

As you read that question, you might have recalled situations where you had to sit through a boring lecture or read an uninspired text. You might also have thought about a particularly engaging teacher or a particular conference session where the speaker got everyone in the room revved up and involved.

There are tricks to the trade. These days, live polling and *"gamification"* are becoming standard practices in education and in the training business. These techniques improve retention and comprehension by engaging a person's mind in the process of answering questions and solving problems.

Your role as a leader/teacher/mentor is not to solve every problem for your followers and students and clients ...

... is it?

Absolutely not; your role is to ask guiding questions and create challenges and tests that expand people's talents, skills and abilities.

I recently read a report about an experiment where a group of college students were given a test before any exposure to the course material.

They were literally set up to fail!

The control group went through the expected learning process; they read the assignment then took the test. The subject group took the test first, then read the assignments.

As expected, the subject group failed miserably—the first time they took the test.

They were then given a second test, similar, but not identical to the first.

The second time around they outperformed the control group significantly. Exposing the students to the questions first helped them focus on finding specific solutions. This process helped them retain the course material to a much higher degree.

You could say they just knew what was expected of them. I'm sure that has a lot to do with it, but I also know from experience that asking the question first initiates a much more focused thinking process.

I know this because we've been teaching martial arts this way for centuries!

I remember taking a lesson with a master I greatly admired. He asked me to show him some of the techniques I was working on, especially any that were giving me trouble.

As I did the techniques, he started asking me questions.

Why was I striking to a particular target? Why was I approaching from a particular angle? What would I do if the attacker approached from a different angle?

I had driven almost two hours for this lesson, and believe me, it wasn't cheap either. I started to get a little aggravated—after all, wasn't I coming here seeking his wisdom?

I wanted answers, not more problems! Suddenly it hit me.

Master knew the answers, but if he just gave me the quick

fix, I probably wouldn't have remembered a damn thing. Instead, he guided me through a process of analyzing the problem and testing a variety of possible solutions. Instead of just spouting out information, he was then able to validate or question my work, depending on what I needed, and guide me to an even higher level of analysis and performance.

Earlier I shared the teaching of the renowned Kenpo master Professor Nick Cerio—remember his words?

He said that earning a black belt was simply the development of a good learning attitude. By earning a black belt, you learn how to learn.

How can anyone learn how to learn if you just give them all the answers?

OK—but there are times when it's necessary to just bear down and present the facts. Sometimes you've got to do a straight forward presentation of information.

Putting aside the license I'm taking in this section, you'd probably consider it pretty annoying if this book were peppered with questions after every paragraph.

If you want that information to stick, especially when you're face to face, find strategic places to insert a question.

Rhetorical questions are effective too—anything that shifts a person's mindset from a passive to an active gear ...

... Does that make sense?

(That's the one I use as a fall-back!)

I remember struggling with a particular technique when I had a lesson scheduled with one of my Masters. When the lesson started, I asked him some questions about the technique. It involved a complicated throw and I just wasn't getting it.

Master asked me how many times I'd practiced the technique. I told him a hundred or so—something in that range.

He said, "Keep practicing. Ask me your question after you've done it 1,000 times."

What the hell was I paying these guys for?

I saw him again a few months later. He said, "Last time I was here, didn't you have a question for me?"

I said, "I did, but I forgot what it was!"

He then asked me how many times I'd practiced the technique since our last lesson.

I told him at least 1,000, probably more, just like he told me to do.

Then he said:

"You didn't forget. You answered the question."

Isn't that a powerful way to teach?

TEACHING IS SHARING

"The Excellent person is the teacher of the person who is not Excellent,

"The person who is not Excellent is the material for the Excellent person."

~Lao Tzu

Above all, teaching is sharing—sharing your knowledge, wisdom and experience.

I sincerely believe that leadership is the highest form of human expression.

Teaching is the highest expression of leadership.

I said earlier that power only expands through sharing.

Your power as a leader is determined by your ability to cultivate the power of others. Your power as a leader expands by helping other people take the trip as well—by helping them become more powerful.

Imagine an organization where everyone is dedicated to continual self-improvement and where they are inspired and encouraged to share their experience with others.

This isn't some kind of metaphysical exercise; I see this idea in action every day in my life as a Sensei. I see the power in this mindset in people from age three to grizzled old guys. This power transcends age, gender, and every other imaginable demographic.

Take a group of people and nourish their capacity for growth and self-perfection, and you've got a dynamic and powerful group of people. Encourage them to teach others along the way, and you've got a group whose impact will last for generations.

What would this mindset do for your organization or business?

Business power expands exponentially through teaching.

The great teacher and pioneer of modern business training, John H. Patterson, once said:

*"*BUSINESS IS NOTHING BUT TEACHING.*"*

Teach effectively and the power of your organization multiplies. Embed this philosophy of teaching and sharing in your organization's culture.

Develop peer to peer mentoring. Turn everyone in your organization into a teacher / leader.

One of the great benefits of teaching is that the teacher often learns as much if not more than the student.

Once again I call on one of my heroes, Ben Franklin:

*"*TELL ME AND I FORGET. TEACH ME AND I REMEMBER. INVOLVE ME AND I LEARN.*"*

The more involved your people are in this process, the more you expand their power as individuals. The more involved they are with helping one another grow, the stronger the bonds that create a powerful organization.

Still, some people try to protect turf.

The effective leader does not protect turf—he expands his power by developing others with the skills and abilities to make his vision a reality.

Once more from Manz and Sims:

> Leading others to lead themselves is the key to tapping the intelligence, the spirit, the creativity, the commitment, and most of all the tremendous unique potential of each individual.

You do that by sharing.

Why do so many leaders feel the need to protect turf?

They may be jealous or worried that someone is going to knock them off their perch. These folks may need some development in the confidence department.

If you're willing to develop your skills as a true Master, there will always be room for you at the top—it's the middle and the bottom that are crowded!

You should be training someone to take your place; how else can you move up?

Train your replacement so you can move on to bigger and better things.

The genuine leader does not preserve his position by keeping other people down, he strengthens his position by lifting them up.

I started Northern Chi with a small group of *Ronin*—masterless warriors. I recognized the need to establish one of us as the ranking martial artist in our organization. I knew that while I was ready, or at least willing to serve as the administrator, I would not hold the highest martial arts rank.

That role would go to Master Chris Keith.

One of Master Keith's most important jobs was to guide the proctors at every Black Belt test. Rookie Black Belts serving as proctors are usually champing at the bit, eager to torture the next group of candidates as enthusiastically as they remember being tortured.

Ironically, the more recently the new Black Belt has tested, the less accurate the recollection of the ordeal. Ask any new Black Belt about the test, and you'll get a greatly exaggerated account.

Don't get me wrong, a Black Belt test is certainly just that—a serious test. But if we've done our jobs as Sensei right and prepared our students properly, it shouldn't be a day for eliminating unworthy candidates; it should be a day for our candidates to discover their true potential. Our job on test day is to provide the best possible conditions for our students to test themselves under fire—and succeed.

At one particular test, our newest group of proctors were

a bit over-zealous. Master Keith and I overheard their plans for how tough they were going to be on today's group. They were gossiping about the shortcomings of some of the candidates. Some even expressed doubts that this new group was as tough or as worthy as they were. The previous generation always seems a little softer—right?

Master Keith called all the instructors together. Then he said:

> Our job is to test the candidate in a way that leaves no doubt that he has achieved victory over something. What each candidate has to overcome: their own doubts about themselves and their resistance to our commands.

> The candidates will bond, at least for today, into a group, an army that is doing battle against us.

> This will be an honest battle, and we will do nothing to destroy the candidate's self-confidence.

> Together they'll do battle against the instructors—and THEY will emerge victorious!"

In that moment, Master Keith embodied everything special about being the Sensei—and the Leader.

A genuine leader answers two simple callings and they both involve sharing:

First—be your best; lead by example. This is sharing your Self.

Then—inspire others to be their best.

Share the same opportunities you had. Share the challenges that will help them grow and prepare them to face those challenges with the highest potential for success.

Sharing defines the true teacher, the genuine leader—the Sensei.

8. LEAD BY SHARING, NOT ACCUMULATING

"THE WISE MAN DOES NOT LAY UP HIS OWN TREASURES. THE MORE HE GIVES TO OTHERS, THE MORE HE HAS FOR HIS OWN."

~LAO TZU

Share unconditionally—with no expectation of return.

You grow as a leader, and as a person, in direct proportion to what you're willing to share with others. You bring out the best in others not because you expect anything from them, but because you're willing to extend your best self first.

Everything is backwards today ...

People demand respect before they offer it. They only love when they think they'll get love in return. They feel entitled to a certain price for their presence before they prove their value.

It's fair and reasonable to expect a return in some areas.

You should expect to be paid for your work. You should also expect to compensate others for the time, goods and services you get from them. True freedom depends on the opportunity for each party to benefit from these exchanges, and it's right to expect those benefits when you are trading tangible goods and delivering true value.

On the other hand, there are certain things that only expand through sharing. In these areas, you only receive when you're willing to give—and you receive the most when you expect nothing in return.

Three things you should give unconditionally are love, respect, and wisdom.

You expand your power as a leader by expanding the power of your followers. You do this by teaching and by sharing your love, respect, and wisdom unconditionally. You've got to trust that people will take what you give them and do something useful with it, whether it comes back to you directly or not.

What you can teach and what you are willing to share are your most valuable resources as a leader.

SHARE POWER

Your own power, your effectiveness as a leader, only expands through sharing.

Shelley Kirkpatrick and Edwin Locke explain in an article quoted in The Leader's Companion:

> ... power is an 'expandable pie,' not a fixed sum; effective leaders give power to others as a means of increasing their own power. Effective leaders do not see power as something that is competed for but rather as something that can be distributed to followers without detracting from their own power.

There is nothing more inspiring to your followers than your commitment to help them become more powerful.

The source of all human power resides in the body, mind and spirit.

You'd think this would be common sense—you've got to take care of yourself in body, mind and spirit if you want to be happy and successful and perform to your full potential.

To share the power, you've got to share the source. You've got to provide the support and resources for people to develop in body, mind and spirit.

I ring this bell again and again, personal development and professional performance are inseparable. If you want people to perform effectively, develop the person.

Why do so many leaders fail to support and invest in the personal development of the people who serve their organizations, *especially in mind and spirit?*

I think this is because it's so difficult to measure an exact return on investment in these areas. As difficult at it is to measure, the negative impact you get when you don't invest in these areas is frightening.

The cost of not sharing the power—of not developing people in these source areas, does eventually show up on your bottom line.

This expense shows up in the form of diminished performance, disengagement, surging health care expenses and lost time. It shows up in the costs of replacing under-inspired employees and leaders who leave in search of better opportunities so they can seek their true potential.

For American businesses, these losses amount to billions of dollars every year.

What is your share of that cost?

SUPPORT THE BODY

The data is indisputable—healthy people are simply more productive.

Invest in proactive health initiatives and you reduce sick time, health insurance costs, injuries and lawsuits.

It's that simple.

SUPPORT THE MIND

Support your people emotionally and invest in both their personal and professional development.

People who are supported emotionally are much more productive too. They are more engaged and far less likely to waste time. They're also far more creative and better equipped to solve problems and deal with adversity.

People who feel supported in their personal and professional development stay longer and they work harder when they're with you.

Be proactive in identifying people's talents and cultivating their best talents. Give them opportunities to grow. Cultivate and encourage strong networks, peer support and productive group dynamics.

SUPPORT THE SPIRIT

This is where you share vision, meaning and purpose.

You want more engaged people?

Give them a clear purpose and share a meaningful vision that works for both the individual and the organization.

Want to measure this?

Call it "spiritual capital." You'll see spiritual capital in the form of loyalty, dedication and full engagement.

If you want to lead a powerful organization, you've got to share the power. You do this by developing people—in body, mind and spirit.

SHARE AUTHORITY

You can't do it all by yourself, and people rise to much higher levels of performance when they have more autonomy and control over their own work.

Give people the authority and the resources they need to create and implement the solutions that will resolve the current challenge.

I know I quote Patton a lot. I have my reasons—here's one of them:

> "NEVER TELL PEOPLE HOW TO DO THINGS. TELL THEM WHAT TO DO AND THEY WILL SURPRISE YOU WITH THEIR INGENUITY."

SHARE THE CREDIT

Another of my favorite Patton quotes:

> "A GENERAL OFFICER WHO WILL INVARIABLY ASSUME THE RESPONSIBILITY FOR FAILURE, WHETHER HE DESERVES IT OR NOT, AND INVARIABLY GIVE THE CREDIT FOR SUCCESS TO OTHERS, WHETHER THEY DESERVE IT OR NOT, WILL ACHIEVE OUTSTANDING SUCCESS."

People want to be recognized for their efforts. They want credit when their work produces results and when their contributions are part of a greater success.

SHARE THE WEALTH!

Studies continually show that financial incentives like bonuses are less motivating than a sense of purpose, autonomy and trust.

Don't use that data to justify behaving like a Scrooge.

Money may not be the most important incentive, but it is still important. The flip side is how demotivating it is when the team pitches in to drive profits and the owner scoops up all the chips.

So yes ... when efforts yield profits, share the wealth!

As I said, certain things should be shared unconditionally, with absolutely no expectation of return. This includes spiritual resources like love, respect, courage, compassion and wisdom. Any attempt to measure a direct return on investment in these areas is nothing but an exercise in frustration.

Material resources can be measured directly, and you should measure them.

Spiritual resources are infinite—material resources are not!

What's important here is that you clearly define the parameters for sharing material wealth. People need to know they can expect fair compensation for their work and that they've got a stake in the organization's success. There is nothing more discouraging and de-motivating than to work hard to help the company produce a windfall only to see leadership reward themselves with bonuses while the people at the front lines are cut out of the bounty.

Dan Pink and others have clearly demonstrated that money is usually not the strongest motivator, and material incentives have only a limited effect on individual performance—but there's a caveat.

Money is a poor incentive only once a person's basic material expectations are met. Until and unless a person feels he's treated fairly, money matters—*a lot*.

I'll take another page from Sam Walton's playbook:

> Share your profits with all your associates, and treat them as partners. In turn, they will treat you as a partner, and together you will all perform beyond your wildest expectations.

Worked pretty well for him.

Once again it's simple; don't over-complicate it. When the people who work for you help increase your wealth—share it.

SHARE SUCCESS

Success is the goal that gives our lives meaning and purpose. Of course, that depends on exactly how you define success.

There is no "my success" when you're a leader. It's our success.

I've become a cocky old bastard in some regards. Just after I turned 50, I proclaimed that I now know exactly what success is. When I make this declaration during a keynote or in a workshop, I can start a fight—and that's a fight I'm willing to start!

I can and will define success for you…

Success is simply feeling that you have enough— materially, emotionally and spiritually.

That's it.

The fight usually starts when someone stands up to tell me that I can't define what success means to anyone else.

Well—*I just did.*

What I did not do is tell you how much is "enough." That's completely up to you. I wouldn't presume to tell anyone else how much they need to feel satisfied and successful.

I do, however, know this as a fact: when you don't feel as if you have enough, you *cannot* feel successful. You may even feel depressed or desperate.

Poverty is *not* an empowering experience.

There are some problems with success that make it elusive, changeable and sometimes difficult to recognize, even when you're apparently successful.

First—Success is not a fixed point.

It's difficult if not impossible for most people to identify a specific amount of money, a particular achievement, or even an ideal life partner that absolutely guarantees success.

Next—Success is a feeling, and by definition, it's impossible to objectively quantify a feeling.

Feelings are also extremely dynamic and fluid and sometimes subject to external forces beyond your control.

The good news is that while feelings and emotions are difficult if not impossible to control, you can always control your response to them. Your response can in turn alter and shape your perceptions and feelings.

Finally—Success is not about getting more—it's about having enough.

Enough doesn't mean you need to have more than someone else, but unfortunately, that's exactly how most people measure success—and that can leave you sadly disappointed.

As a leader, your success is dependent upon the success of your followers. When they fail—you fail. When they're suffering—you suffer too. Of course, the upside is that when they are successful—you are also successful.

Having said that, an effective leader develops followers—not dependent children.

You are *not* solely responsible for each person's individual success or failure.

Your success as a leader, however, grows in direct proportion to your willingness to share that responsibility and in direct proportion to your investment in the success of each individual you serve.

Show your people that you are truly committed to their success. That's how you inspire your followers to create the abundance that defines success—for themselves, for the organization, and for you.

In the end, success is something you and your followers produce together.—share it.

JUST SHARE

One of the leaders I admire most is a neighbor of mine. Well, it would be more accurate to say that he once lived just a couple of blocks from where I do now.

Unless you're a serious Civil War buff, you might not know Joshua Chamberlain. He was almost lost to history until his memory was resurrected in Michael Shaara's *The Killer Angels* and later in the movie *Gettysburg*, which introduced Chamberlain to a new generation.

Chamberlain left a promising career at Bowdoin College to petition for a commission to serve in the Union Army. He would become a hero at Gettysburg.

At the end of the war, he was chosen to accept the surrender of the Confederate troops at Appomattox where his decision to salute the Southern army earned him a place in history as one of our most compassionate—and controversial leaders. While his gesture angered some people in the North, it was greatly appreciated by the Southern troops and played a large part in healing the wounds of war on both sides.

After the war, Chamberlain served as governor of Maine and was a very popular speaker at Civil War reunions and other commemorative events. This is from his speech at the 100th anniversary of Lincoln's birth:

"GREAT CRISES IN HUMAN AFFAIRS CALL OUT THE GREAT IN MEN. BUT TRUE GREATNESS IS NOT IN NOR OF THE SINGLE SELF; IT IS OF THAT LARGER PERSONALITY, THAT SHARED AND SHARING LIFE WITH OTHERS, IN WHICH, EACH GIVING OF HIS BEST FOR THEIR BETTERMENT, WE ARE GREATER THAN OURSELVES ..."

Look for opportunities for sharing.

Sharing is the action of expanding power. Through sharing, each of us becomes greater than any one of us alone.

Your effectiveness as a leader is enhanced by your capacity

and willingness to share. When you inspire others to share, you expand the power of the group—exponentially.

I can sum up everything I know about leadership in one simple phrase:

Leadership is sharing—a leader shares.

5 Tactics

If strategy is what you're going to do, then tactics are how you're going to do it.

Martial artists and leaders can benefit greatly by studying tactics. Over the years, I've found that every useful tactic and technique can fit into one of these 5 basic categories:

OPPOSITION

DEFLECTION

LEVERAGE (CONCENTRATION)

BORROWING

HARMONY

I started my martial arts adventure in a system called Shaolin Kenpo Karate. That compound name implies that Kenpo is a hybrid system—a combination of several traditions with contributions from Masters in many different cultures, but primarily Japanese, Chinese, and Okinawan.

Later in my career, I became fascinated with Taiji, Qigong, and Chin Na. I also started training with people who practiced other systems including Tae Kwon Do, Shotokan, and Aikido.

Just to complicate things even further, I decided to satisfy what today would be called a "bucket list" ambition and joined a boxing gym.

Believe me, I've heard some glorious arguing and chest thumping by one master or another about the superiority of this system or the other—this technique or that.

After a while, I came to the conclusion that I'd rather be the dumbest guy in the room.

That is, while the Great Masters pounded their chests and argued over which system, strategy or technique was best, I'd keep my eyes and ears open and my mouth shut and simply try to steal what I could use from all of them.

By the way, a lot of these ethnocentric experts were wearing orange and purple belts.

It's funny how the people with the least experience can sometimes be the most opinionated.

Fortunately for me, I found teachers who were much more open minded. These Masters would look above the skirmish to see the whole field.

Dr. Yang, Jwing-Ming was one of the best.

Dr. Yang's background includes a mix of various arts, both hard and soft styles. Even more important, he was trained both in traditional arts and in science.

His doctorate is in electrical engineering. That gives him a wonderful deductive capacity when it comes to understanding the arts and an ability to discern what is real and what is, well—crap.

I often talk about Dr. Yang as a martial artist, a teacher, and as one of today's most insightful living philosophers. Whenever and wherever I do, I say that in the bridge between East and West—Dr. Yang is the strongest plank!

He's a very strong plank in the bridge between traditional and contemporary as well.

Martial artists, like business people, often struggle with the desire to innovate versus a strong attachment to tradition. You might remember a story I told you earlier in which Dr. Yang addresses this conflict:

"Just because it's old—doesn't make it right."

Tradition is important, and it's vital that we honor and keep the principles, values and wisdom of the past—if it works.

We too often cast aside valuable tradition. Way too often we fall into Edmund Burke's infamous trap, "Those who cannot remember the past are doomed to repeat it."

On the other hand, we also too often cling to obsolete traditions even though we know there's a better way.

Admiral Grace Hopper stated the problem clearly:

"THE MOST DANGEROUS PHRASE IN THE LANGUAGE IS:

"WE'VE ALWAYS DONE IT THIS WAY."

Innovation involves risk—Creativity requires courage

Dr. Yang taught me to how to distinguish between vestigial and viable tradition. He helped me see beyond any one style or system and how to analyze the fundamentals that underlie all effective techniques and tactics.

Like the Masters I admired, I became a reductionist.

If I could find the most fundamental elements of a technique or tactic, I knew I could make it work in a variety of applications. If I could keep it simple, my recall and reaction would be much quicker and effective.

Works in leadership too!

In regard to techniques and tactics, I came to some powerful realizations. First of all, what we're ultimately looking for in any technique is power—our capacity to perform effectively.

Remember that the source of human power resides in body, mind and spirit. If you want to be powerful, to perform effectively, you've got to cultivate each area.

You generate power through *motivation and discipline* over

time. Yes—it takes time to develop power.

You apply power most efficiently when you master *balance, focus* and *timing.*

Understand these simple ideas, and you can find the power in any technique, in fighting or in leadership.

Apply these fundamental concepts and you will become more powerful—as a person and as a leader.

Once I started to understand these fundamentals, it became much easier to understand, learn and assimilate techniques and tactics from various systems and teachers.

When I want to access the potential power of any technique, I look for where I can isolate and improve balance, focus and timing. I find ways to practice those elements for each technique.

Isolating the fundamental elements of power in each leadership style eliminates any gap in understanding between various strategies, techniques and tactics.

Through this process I became more open and receptive to new ideas. This process also helped me evolve and mature to be far less threatened by outside ideas and other instructors.

(And yes—this works in leadership too!)

As I became more confident and open minded, I started to host other instructors and bring them in for seminars so my students could learn directly from the Masters.

At one such event, I was practicing with one of my star pupils, Paul.

The guest instructor was teaching a leverage technique. Instead of being as engaged as I was, I noticed Paul was getting a bit agitated—even irritated. I asked "What's up?"

"Sensei, *all this guy is doing is Combination 3!*"

Our Combinations are sets of techniques we teach to study and practice various tactics and situations. Paul had recognized the similarity between what our guest was teaching and what he was already practicing. The only problem was that he saw this as a problem.

I said, "Paul, that's great! Now that you see the similarities, you can appreciate the differences!"

Each master has his own unique twist on any particular technique. That's why we call them martial "artists." We should apply the same designation to leadership study.

Isn't leadership as much art as science?

I continued, "If you couldn't understand how that technique is similar to yours, you wouldn't even notice the subtle differences."

I explained that most of the students in the room had their hands full just trying to learn the specific technique. If they didn't grasp the similarity, they simply didn't have the capacity to see and apply any subtle differences—and those differences are what make any basic technique or process more effective.

As your capacity for observation grows, so does your capacity to elevate your technique and adapt your technique to a wider range of applications.

"STRATEGY REQUIRES THOUGHT, TACTICS REQUIRE OBSERVATION."

~MAX EUWE

I've learned to look at any new technique by first identifying any core similarity with anything I've already learned or experienced. I isolate the fundamentals—then I look for any differences to see if I can steal some new "chops."

This is exactly what I've done with the 5 *Tactics*.

I've found through experience that nearly every technique I've learned in martial arts can be categorized under one of these 5 *Tactics*.

As I look for the underlying power in each tactic, I can analyze any technique for its effectiveness and understand its most basic—most powerful application.

Experience taught me that nearly every leadership technique—nearly every interaction you have with the people you lead—falls into one of these tactical areas too.

I've come to a point where I teach tactics far more than I do techniques. The problem with techniques is that there's just too damn many of them! (*It's probably better to say—you've got plenty to choose from.*)

Tactics help you recognize and apply the right techniques.

TACTICS DICTATE TECHNIQUES

Let's say I'm fighting a much bigger and stronger opponent…

You can't fight strength with strength.

Other things being equal, size and strength are great advantages in a fight. If someone is bigger and stronger, you've got to find a way to counter that advantage.

As you'll soon see, oppositional tactics won't work in this situation. I can't fight an overwhelming force with direct force. I've got to apply the tactics of deflection, leverage, or borrowing.

Within each of those tactics, there are any number of techniques available. However, if you apply techniques for force on force encounters to a situation that requires leverage tactics, they simply won't work.

You've got to apply the techniques that best apply to the tactical opportunities in any given situation.

One of the great weaknesses of ineffective leadership is an unwillingness to adjust one's thinking—being close minded to change.

When you understand tactics, you are better able to choose the right technique for each situation and adapt your tactics and techniques for changing conditions.

"BE LIKE WATER MAKING ITS WAY THROUGH CRACKS. DO NOT BE ASSERTIVE, BUT ADJUST TO THE OBJECT, AND YOU SHALL FIND A WAY AROUND OR THROUGH IT. IF NOTHING WITHIN YOU STAYS RIGID, OUTWARD THINGS WILL DISCLOSE THEMSELVES.

"EMPTY YOUR MIND, BE FORMLESS. SHAPELESS, LIKE WATER. IF YOU PUT WATER INTO A CUP, IT BECOMES THE CUP. YOU PUT WATER INTO A BOTTLE AND IT BECOMES THE BOTTLE. YOU PUT IT IN A TEAPOT, IT BECOMES THE TEAPOT. NOW, WATER CAN FLOW OR IT CAN CRASH ...

" ... BE WATER, MY FRIEND."

~BRUCE LEE

OPPOSITION

When we talk about opposition, we're talking about pure force—mano a mano.

There are two major oppositional tactics. One is the tactic of the bull—when you go head to head with the opposition.

The other is to hold your ground—to establish and defend your position to the last full measure.

In a punch or kick or a direct block, our objective is to create a powerful impact force. We're literally throwing one object into another—like the charging bulls.

When two objects meet head to head, the one with the most force wins.

Force is the product of mass and acceleration. The faster you strike and the more mass you throw at the target, the greater the force. You can increase the power of the strike by increasing mass or acceleration.

When you hold your ground—you're not moving at all. You've got no choice but to increase mass in whatever context that might apply.

Force on force opposition is expensive—in battle or in business.

JIM BOUCHARD

From *The Art of War* ...

"THE RULE IS THAT IF YOU OUTNUMBER YOUR ENEMY TEN TO ONE, SURROUND THEM;

"FIVE TO ONE, ATTACK ..."

Sun Tzu is telling us that opposing the enemy by force requires a serious commitment of resources. You need 5 to 1 odds to effectively throw yourself into a direct assault. You need 10 to 1 odds if you're going to wait your enemy out!

Despite how expensive or inconvenient it might be, sometimes you've got to go head to head and sometimes you've got to hold your position.

The most important place you've got to stand fast is in defense of your core values and principles.

In his book *No-Compromise Leadership,* my friend Neil Ducoff writes:

> Tampering with the values of a business is much like tampering with the forces of nature. Compromise values anywhere in your company and minute changes, often called the butterfly effect, can cause a tidal wave of otherwise unavoidable issues, problems and drama.

Tactics are specific to particular conditions and circumstances. You must know when to flow like water and when to stand like a mountain.

242

When it comes to your values and principles—you must be a rock.

Another area where direct opposition is the appropriate tactic is in dealing with bad characters.

You've got to attack these enemies face to face. Hesitate to commit yourself to this fight and you risk losing the trust of good people who count on you to have the courage to stand up.

In our age of runaway political correctness, leaders too often placate the worst people in an organization—usually out of fear of political reprisal or legal entanglement.

Get over it!

Christine Pearson and Christine Porath present the butcher's bill in stark detail in their book, *The Cost of Bad Behavior.*

Let's just start with this—according to their research, 12 percent of workers leave their jobs annually because they were treated with disrespect and incivility by other people in the organization, quite often by a supervisor:

Average price of replacing each of those employees: $50,000.

Annual cost of job stress to U.S. corporations: $300 billion.

Amount of time Fortune 1000 executives spend resolving employee conflicts: **7 WEEKS per year.** *(Emphasis mine.)*

In one particularly compelling case study Pearson and Porath detail the efforts of Cisco Systems to analyze the cost of incivility in their company. Cisco is consistently rated as one of the best places to work—a model of civility!

Still, Cisco found that:

> The organization wide costs for potential time lost by targets who worried about additional uncivil incidents and future interactions with offenders totaled nearly $2 million per year. With estimates for the costs of weakened commitment (also calculated as lost productivity value) and job changes (calculated on the basis of cost per hire) added in, the total topped $8 million.

The authors add that this is not the ultimate cost. It's just the "starting point" and doesn't include secondary costs!

You may not run a global corporation like Cisco. For the small business person, the cost in proportion to the total output of the business may be even more devastating.

If you have four employees, what is the impact of losing one good employee because you don't want to go up against the company jerk?

The damage does not stop there.

Even more disturbing is the cost to the individual. Being subjected to incivility and disrespect actually alters your brain chemistry.

"It seems that whether the snake is in the garden or in the next cubicle, flight or fight responses kick in." Unchecked, this condition can destroy your health. "Incivility may spark an effect similar to post-traumatic stress disorder."

This damage is lasting and, untreated, can leave an indelible mark on the targeted person's life.

Unfortunately, top performers and even bosses are too often the culprits. You must find the courage to oppose any bad actors in your organization. Sometimes you've just got to throw yourself in their path, force on force.

It is your responsibility as a leader to place the needs of followers above or at least in equal position to your own.

I'll argue that the needs of your followers and yours—are one and the same.

DEFLECTION

Deflection is often more efficient and effective than opposition. *In Tai Chi Secrets of the Ancient Masters,* Dr. Yang, Jwing-Ming translates one of the *Taiji Classics:*

> No matter if he uses enormous power to attack me, I use four ounces to lead him aside, deflecting his one thousand pounds.

Dr. Yang adds:

> If you try to make a sudden, major change in the course of an incoming attack, you might get bowled over by the forward momentum. Even if you succeeded, you would need to expend considerable force.

With my martial arts students, I always use the example of trying to stop an incoming punch ...

A skilled fighter can through a punch with about 1,200 pound of force. This means that if you want to stop it dead, you need at least 1,200 pounds of resistance. To push it back—you need even more.

Just remember that a collision creates an additive result. Add your 1,200 pounds to your opponents 1,200 and you have 2,400 pounds of impact!

That can create quite a painful physics problem.

It requires far less force to deflect the strike from the side—away from the direction of the oncoming force.

HOW CAN YOU APPLY THIS PRINCIPLE IN LEADERSHIP?

One of the most powerful, effective and readily available deflective tactics available to a leader is—a question.

We've already discussed the power of questions in teaching. A sincere, well placed question can also deflect an aggressive attack and diffuse highly charged emotions.

A good question refocuses the conversation to the aggressor's perspective, not because you're ready to surrender, but to show that you're willing to listen and try and understand.

One persistent challenge in leadership provides the perfect opportunity to apply deflection—when you're dealing with resistance to change.

One of the best techniques for mitigating this resistance, and one that is too seldom used—is to simply ask the people why, specifically, they oppose the change.

Major changes are too often dictated from the top down with little or no input from outside the executive suite.

You'll never come to an understanding by proclamation—understanding starts with a question.

If you want people to "buy in" and support change—start by understanding any concerns they might have.

The very act of asking sincere questions reduces the classic fears and insecurities associated with any significant change. Sometimes people just feel better when they know their concerns are heard and understood.

As you ask questions you may also uncover legitimate reasons for resistance that will help you avoid costly mistakes or lead you to a much more efficient implementation process.

Another useful application deflection is dealing with an angry customer or client.

Faced with a dissatisfied or angry customer, it's typical for a service representative to respond first with opposition. Sometimes this opposition is disguised as a return or refund policy or as an excuse.

Try this next time you're in the line of fire; just ask:

"What would you like to see us do for you?"

You may still have work to do to find a reasonable solution, but just asking the question throws some water on the fire. You're demonstrating to the customer that you have a sincere interest in understanding the problem from their perspective.

It takes a lot of energy to go toe to toe with an angry customer. It takes just a small adjustment in attitude to deflect that anger with a sincere expression of concern.

Deflection is often the most effective tactic for resolving conflict.

Try this tactic next time you have to mediate a highly charged conflict between two co-workers, colleagues and adversaries.

Deflection buys you time—and nothing cools anger better than time.

Rather than fighting when emotions are hot, you schedule the match for a time when both sides can cool down, carefully consider their position, and debate the issue more calmly and rationally.

This is not surrender. It's a tactical redeployment.

You're moving the fight to a more favorable time and better ground. You're positioning your resources to improve the chances of victory—for both sides.

Sun Tzu would be proud.

LISTEN

To master the tactic of deflection, be a good listener.

Listening is a skill. Like any other skill, listening can be learned and cultivated—and you've got to practice! I've coached many managers and business people in listening skills, and it all centers on one thing: *FOCUS.*

You can't force focus—it's a process of letting go. Most of all, you learn to let go of distractions.

The problem is that the human brain is wired for distraction. It's a survival mechanism. We've got to learn how to control that mechanism and turn off the distractions when they're not necessary for survival.

Our ancestors evolved to shift their focus quickly. This quick shift of attention was very useful when they were hunting for their dinner and they heard the low growl of a saber-tooth tiger stalking them from the bushes.

These days, you're not likely to be eaten by a tiger while your attention is focused on listening to someone across your office desk.

When listening, your complete focus needs to be on paying attention to and understanding the person you're listening to.

This sounds basic and should be common sense, however there are a lot of distractions that can interfere with effective listening:

- *Your own agenda*

- *A particular desired outcome*

- *Actual environmental conditions (noise, interruptions)*

- *Personal opinions and beliefs*

- *Time constraints*

- *The urgency or importance of the topic (or lack thereof)*

ELIMINATE OR MITIGATE AS MANY DISTRACTIONS AS POSSIBLE.

With tangible distractions like noise, phones, interruptions, that's pretty simple to do, but some distractions are not as obvious. I call those "intangible distraction." They can be a little harder to squelch.

Intangible distractions include:

- *Prejudices or entrenched beliefs*

- *Stress*

- *Outside pressures*

- *Fear or sense of threat*

- *Deception or lack of transparency*

Any of these conditions can steal your attention from where it belongs—on the person you're listening to.

One of the most difficult intangible distractions to manage is—your opinion.

You need to practice putting aside your opinion in the moment. When you're listening, your own opinions are not the priority. Productive listening is receptive, not reactive.

It's difficult to keep quiet when someone says something you disagree with; however, the time for response is later. When you show a sincere interest in listening, your considered response carries much more weight than a reactionary opinion—whether you agree or not.

One of the worst distractions is time—or lack of it.

Schedule time for listening. Your goal here is not a conversation—it's simply to make time to listen.

Make sure the other person knows in advance how much time you can commit to listening. This allows you to pay full attention without worrying about any other agenda.

And as to the agenda ...

You may want or need a specific outcome. For example, you may need someone to buy in to a new company policy or you may need to make a sale.

In the listening phase, your desired outcome is a distraction.

Practice putting it aside. Make your short term objective simply to gather information. This gives you the information you need to respond much more effectively.

My friend Dave is a Master salesman. The funny thing is, I've never heard him try to sell anything.

I've been on several sales calls with Dave where he hardly opened his mouth—he listened.

I'm sure there were times when Dave needed his commission to make the mortgage or put shoes on one of his six kids—you'd never know it. His focus is always solely on his customer's needs and he understands what his customer needs—because he *listens.*

Not surprisingly, Dave is one of the most successful people I know, and one of the leaders I most admire.

I once heard that the greatest gift you can give another human being is your attention.

That's what listening is all about. It's about the gift of paying full attention to someone else.

LEVERAGE

In physics and fighting, leverage is using mechanical advantage to amplify input energy to produce an exponential increase in power.

In leadership, your lever is the mind, and you're looking for psychological rather than mechanical advantage.

Inspiration and motivation are good levers for a leader. Through inspiration, you can leverage the skills, talents and energies of many people to produce a far greater result than what can be accomplished by any individual working alone.

Opposition and deflection are almost always responsive tactics. That is, we most often employ those tactics in response to some immediate threat or attack.

Leverage, borrowing and harmony can often be employed proactively.

Be on the lookout constantly for opportunities to apply leverage and these higher tactics to innovate, create new opportunities, and expand the power of the people you serve.

Like a good Sensei, I'm revealing each of these tactics in order of the increasing level of understanding, skill, and mastery you need to employ each one effectively ...

IT TAKES WILL, NOT SKILL, TO STAND IN OPPOSITION

It takes much greater skill to apply a leverage tactic.

Chin Na is the Chinese fighting art of leverage: seizing, locking, throwing and employing concentrated attacks against specific vulnerable targets. Much of what I learned about leverage, in martial arts and in real life, came from my experiences with Dr. Yang, Jwing-Ming and the study of Chin Na.

Dr. Yang wrote the bible in this style: *Comprehensive Applications of Shaolin Chin Na*. In it he says:

CHIN NA MUST RESPOND TO AND
FOLLOW THE SITUATION;
TECHNIQUES MUST BE SKILLFUL, ALIVE,
FAST AND POWERFUL.

Couldn't we just substitute the word "leadership" in place of "Chin Na"?

As I said, this tactic demands a higher level of awareness, skill and experience.

You need expert focus and timing to apply these techniques effectively.

Dr. Yang adds:

"IT IS USUALLY MUCH EASIER TO STRIKE
AN OPPONENT THAN TO CONTROL HIM."

LEVERAGE IS ABOUT CONTROL

Dr. Yang told us about a trip he made to Russia to teach seminars in Chin Na and Taiji. One of his hosts on that trip gave him a ball cap with a saying in Russian embroidered across the front. It read, *"Pinky Collector."*

They were honoring Dr. Yang for his ability to control a much larger man by using a leverage technique against his smallest digit!

You can try this—*carefully!*

(I'll state for the record that I am not liable for you injuring or maiming yourself in this experiment!)

Anyway, gently pry your pinky back. You'll soon notice a point where this becomes extremely uncomfortable, then painful.

Applied properly, you can lift a 300 man to his toes or drive him to his knees by the skillful application of leverage on the pinky.

I still use this trick in demonstrations all the time. I start by picking a large, rugged-looking guy out of the audience and asking: "Do you believe I can get this guy to dance on his toes using just one hand?"

Of course people are skeptical, but the physiology behind the experiment is really quite simple.

By applying even a small force against an extremely sensitive part of the body, even a big tough guy becomes a lot more cooperative.

I will warn you—it also takes some skill not to snap the poor guy's finger off!

Do not attempt this trick until we train you properly!

Earlier I said that wisdom is the combination of knowledge and experience tempered by awareness.

Know your people and be fully aware of their capabilities, potential and tolerances.

Be fully aware of the conditions and circumstances around you at all times. In self-defense we call this "situational awareness."

Situational awareness is necessary in leadership, too.

In fighting or in leadership, you've got know your surrounding and you've got to be prepared to move first to employ leverage effectively. Otherwise, your adversary will read your intentions and either escape or counter.

LEVERAGE AND CONCENTRATION

Leverage also employs concentrated force.

In Chin Na, we attack specific, vulnerable, highly sensitive targets for maximum effect. Even a small amount of pressure or impact force applied in a concentrated area can produce a highly amplified result.

We call these sensitive areas "pressure points."

In the human body, these are the points where nerves are exposed. This often happens in what we call body cavities, the areas not protected by the heavy armor of bone.

Once again—GENTLY—take one or two fingers and fish for a spot under the hinge of your jaw where you find a very specific spot that feels less than comfortable.

It's not hard to find!

Got it?

This is one of the pressure points we exploit. You'll find others in the arm pit, inside the elbow and knee joints, and over the top of the sternum. The most sensitive and vulnerable cavities of all are the eyes.

If you thought I was going to say groin, well, we go after that too, but an attack to the eyes is still far more frightening and devastating—even if it doesn't invoke quite the same mystique.

The ancient masters even studied various times of day and seasons of the year where specific points are alleged to be even more vulnerable. The only two that made any sense to me were to attack the stomach area just after mid-day, and to attack the kidneys and bladder early in morning.

Do I need to explain further?

I'm very skeptical about the efficacy of some of these claims from a self-defense perspective, but it seems that well-timed application of concentrated force can be a great advantage to the leader.

You can apply concentrated pressure defensively against an aggressor or competitor, or, just as with leverage, concentration can be employed proactively to expand the power of an individual or an organization.

- *Are you focusing your energies where they'll produce the maximum results?*

- *Are you applying your talents and abilities to best advantage?*

- *Are you efficiently utilizing the talents and abilities of others?*

My friend and mentor Joe Calloway is the author of *Being the Best at What Matters Most*.

I asked Joe about the power of concentrating your efforts for best results:

> In business, the most successful aren't those who try and do everything. The most successful are those who do the most important things. Simplicity and clarity are force multipliers.

> Put your efforts and your intention towards doing those handful of things that are truly most important, and your success is sure.

> Don't overthink. Don't complicate. If you can make things simple, you can move mountains.

Give the man a Black Belt!

Leverage is about concentration of power and utilizing force multipliers effectively. It's about amplifying input energy to produce maximum output power.

With the proper application of leverage—you can produce amazing results.

As the ancient sage Archimedes said:

"GIVE ME A PLACE TO STAND, AND A LEVER LONG ENOUGH, AND I WILL MOVE THE WORLD."

BORROWING

The most difficult tactic to master is borrowing. This tactic requires expert balance, focus and timing.

You've got to master control of combined forces—both yours and your attacker's.

Here's how we apply this tactic in self-defense:

Instead of blocking, (opposition), you step inside the arc of a punch, intercepting the strike without diminishing—simply redirecting its power. With expert timing and position, you turn your hips adding your power to energy you borrow from your attacker.

You blend your power with your opponent's and ...

... wham! He's flat on his back.

Whenever I present these tactics in one of my leadership workshops, the idea of borrowing instigates the most discussion and interest.

Borrowing is the art of recognizing and exploiting opportunities to combine the energies of those around you, plus your own, to create an exponentially more powerful outcome.

That is obviously a powerful and attractive concept to a leader!

In our self-defense example, you borrow the physical energy of an attacker. Leaders can borrow energy from an adversary too—but borrowing can also be an effective tactic when you're dealing with entrenched opposition from allies, such as fear of change or resistance to innovation.

You can borrow from the people who are with you as well as those who might be against you.

It's similar to leverage in that you're multiplying force by utilizing material and human resources to the best advantage, but borrowing involves a higher level of understanding, tactical expertise, and timing.

With leverage, you can literally jam a bar under a rock and pry it out.

With borrowing, you've got to position yourself in exactly the right place at exactly the right time—and move in precise harmony with the forces around you.

If I want to borrow the power of my attacker's punch, I'll try to draw him into telegraphing the punch. I want him to throw a big punch—one that will give me more power to use against him!

In leadership—instead of waiting to respond to inevitable opposition, you proactively solicit input from everyone involved.

You want as much participation as possible— that's the energy you're going to borrow.

You also work to cultivate the enthusiasm, creativity and potential of everyone in your organization. Tap into their drive for meaning and purpose.

Look for people early in any process who will give honest feedback and support key decisions along the way—unless they see a better course of action. And if they see a better way, welcome their suggestions and sincerely consider their opinions.

This is similar to leverage—but borrowing expands on leverage. With leverage, you're applying available forces to your best advantage.

In borrowing, your aim is to expand the power of the people involved and help them realize higher and sometimes unexpected levels of contribution and performance. You need to recognize, cultivate and harness their potential—often before they do.

As I said, this borrowing requires expert balance, focus and timing …

Balance—Be well grounded and know as much about what you're proposing and the possible outcomes before you take action.

Stay true to your core values and principles—they serve as the foundation for sustainable growth and innovation.

Focus—Pay attention to all the possible implications and impacts and concentrate your efforts where they will produce the most positive results.

Timing—Understand the right time for every action. Be prepared to adjust to any shifts, reactions or changing conditions and circumstances—in real time.

Harmony

Harmony is really a blend of the other four tactics.

Harmony is truly *"going with the flow."* You operate in a state of active awareness where you recognize threats and opportunities in the moment and respond with the most appropriate tactic and technique—effectively, efficiently and naturally.

Be careful though!

People today just love to turn simple but profound bits of practical philosophy into useless t-shirt slogans and allegedly motivational posters.

"Go with the flow" doesn't mean you're just cork drifting with the current. It's not an excuse for ignorance, laziness or complacency.

Going with the flow requires Mastery ...

It means you've got the skill, experience and awareness to be in complete synergy with the conditions and forces in your space and with the minds and hearts of the people around you—both enemy and ally.

Harmony is only achieved through Mastery.

The legendary Japanese swordsman and strategist Miyamoto Mushashi called this concept, *"Becoming your Opponent."*

You literally try to become of one mind with the people you're leading—and those who may oppose you.

In his *Writings on the Five Elements,* more commonly known as *The Book of Five Rings,* Mushashi teaches:

> In individual strategy, you must have knowledge concerning your opponent's school, discern his personality, and find his strengths and his weaknesses. Use tactics that thwart his intentions, and it is important to seize the initiative of attack by perceiving the rises and falls of your opponent's combativeness and by knowing well the cadences of his intervals. If the strength of your wisdom is sufficient, you can always perceive what the situation is ...

IF YOU ACCURATELY PROBE THE MIND OF YOUR ADVERSARY, YOU WILL FIND MANY WAYS OF WINNING. YOU MUST WORK THIS OUT.

You can see why Musashi's writings are required study for business and leadership students around the world.

Musashi himself would say ...

... study these strategies and tactics well.

PART FOUR
THE SPIRIT OF THE SENSEI LEADER

主領

LEADERSHIP AT ALL LEVELS

Titles, diplomas, ranks and certificates don't make a leader.
Courage, compassion and wisdom do, at any level ...

... at all levels.

A large part of the mindset "gap" in leadership is the tendency to think that only "leaders" can lead.

It does not take formal study or a position of authority to be a leader. There are plenty of extremely knowledgeable people in positions of authority that couldn't lead a monkey to a banana raffle!

Leaders are those people who step up to do what needs to be done—whether they're on the front line or in the corner office.

The spirit of leadership must be embedded in all levels—that's where the real work gets done!

I always think about those old World War II movies where the grizzled sergeant has to take command of the platoon because the green lieutenant can't command the troops.

In those stories, the new lieutenant, fresh out of officer's school, has the training and the authority—but not the experience or credibility to lead effectively under fire.

The battle hardened sergeant is the proven leader.

He has the experience and wisdom. His troops have seen him demonstrate courage under fire. He has already earned the trust and respect of his troops.

The usual plot puts the platoon in some desperate situation. The young lieutenant freezes.

The sergeant leads them through the battle and then, inevitably—someone wants to promote the sergeant—they try to make him an officer!

Of course the sergeant has absolutely no desire to become a commissioned officer.

He has absolutely no ambition to take on the additional administrative duties required of command. He's proud and happy to serve on the front lines.

Isn't the sergeant's leadership every bit as valuable—if not more so in this situation, than the green lieutenant's?

INDEPENDENT OF RANK

AT ANY LEVEL, A LEADER IS:

SOMEONE WHO SEES WHAT NEEDS TO BE
DONE AND DOES IT.

SOMEONE WHO ASKS BEFORE HE'S ASKED.

SOMEONE WHO SEIZES THE OPPORTUNITY
TO SERVE.

Abraham Lincoln was a master storyteller.

According to Donald T. Phillips in *Lincoln on Leadership,*
one of Lincoln's favorite stories to tell involved a Missouri
colonel …

As the colonel organized his regiment, he convinced everyone under his command that he should be the only one in
the unit that would use profanity.

One of the unit's teamsters was a man named John Todd,
who "as roads were not always the best, had some difficulty
in commanding his temper and tongue."

On an especially difficult road, Todd let loose with a volley
of expert cussing:

> The colonel took notice of the offense and brought John
> to account. "John," said he, "didn't you promise to let
> me do all the swearing for the regiment?"

"Yes, I did, Colonel," he replied, "but the fact was the swearing had to be done then or not at all, *and you weren't there to do it.*"

Leadership is your capacity to inspire and lead others— regardless of your position of authority.

Leadership means having the courage to step up first, sometimes without waiting for orders. It's also defined by your willingness to share your knowledge, wisdom and experience with others—no matter what your rank!

Effective leadership is not the product of a 10-step training program. Leadership isn't a one-off. You don't send a team to a weekend retreat and expect them to return as a cadre of freshly minted leaders.

Leadership is a mindset that must be cultivated, encouraged, nurtured and practiced continually at all organizational levels.

The most effective leaders are the people who do without being told, ask before being asked, teach and mentor those around them and most of all—model the behavior they expect from others.

That type of leader may be right in front of you—or right beside you.

LEADERSHIP FOR THE SMALL ORGANIZATION—JUST AS IMPORTANT

Small business operators sometimes think that leadership training is really for the big guys. If you only have a few employees and you know everyone you work with, how important is it to offer structured leadership training, especially to the folks on the front lines?

Leadership is just as important to a local pizza shop as it is to a multi-national corporation. In a small operation, everyone *must* be a leader.

Who else is going to lead?

Leaders are people who take initiative, who can work independently without the constant need for command and control. These are people who ask what needs to be done or, better yet, have it done before being asked. These are the folks who share their knowledge, experience and wisdom freely with their peers.

Most of all, these are people who take personal responsibility for doing their jobs well and people who constantly improve themselves in order to do their jobs better—regardless of whether or not their efforts result in a formal promotion or title.

In a small business, there may not be many opportunities for formal advancement.

If you're the on-site owner with two employees, it's likely that your roles are pretty well established for the long-term.

Don't worry about advancement and titles. Chances are the people working for you aren't worried about those things either—if they were, they'd be working somewhere else.

It's still beneficial to provide your people with leadership training. Over time, this investment will produce consistent and tangible returns.

No matter how small your organization, developing strong leaders at all levels helps each individual grow and become more productive and creative. Better leaders at all levels help the organization operate more effectively and efficiently.

When you commit to developing leaders at all levels—you create the culture of responsiveness and innovation that gives you the ability to take your company to the next level.

WHAT ARE SOME OF THE LEADERSHIP SKILLS AND TRAITS THAT YOU SHOULD CULTIVATE—AT ALL LEVELS?

We've already discussed most of this in regard to your own development as "the leader."

Be sure you extend the opportunity for cultivation to leaders on the front lines too!

THE ABILITY TO THINK AND ACT INDEPENDENTLY

You want people to do what needs to be done when it needs to be done.

You don't want them to clear every decision or action with you—especially when it comes to front line details or areas where they have more knowledge and experience than you do.

You want to cultivate that sense of autonomy that leverages effectiveness and inspires peak performance.

THE ABILITY TO MENTOR PEERS

The culture of any business depends on the ability and willingness of individuals to share knowledge and experience and mentor peers.

You want people who teach, share and cultivate one another's strengths and who recognize and correct their own weaknesses.

THE COURAGE TO ACT IN THE MOMENT

Along with the ability to act independently, it's essential that people know they can act with your full support to best serve the interests of your organization, your business and your customers.

You need to be supportive of this independence even in times when the short term results are not what you may have hoped for.

YOU DON'T HAVE TO GO IT ALONE

One of the complaints I hear most often from small business operators is that they sometimes have to do everything by themselves.

You won't have this problem when you commit yourself to developing leaders at all levels!

No matter how small or how big your business, the key to freeing your time and energy to move your business forward is knowing you can depend on the people working for you.

You achieve this freedom by training leaders— at all levels.

I once operated an association of five martial arts centers. This was a very small operation. I owned two centers with only three employees. The other centers were independent owner/operators either flying solo or with one or two partners.

I always felt that the only way our small business could effectively serve our members and students was to continually develop our *"Leadership Team,"* the name we adopted for both professional owners and managers and volunteer instructors.

We held monthly meetings to work on business issues and to provide both personal and professional development to the instructors and managers—in addition to their martial arts training.

I can't tell you how many times the instructors and center directors thanked me for conducting these meetings. These events were an important factor in building our organization and cementing the bonds that made us a strong team.

These meetings also provided me with a great deal of support. It afforded me direct and unfiltered contact with everyone in the organization. They in turn showed me where my leadership was working—and where I needed more work!

Most of all, these meetings continually reminded me—I was not going it alone!

"KEEP FRIENDSHIP WITH ONE ANOTHER ..."

If you run a small business, you're shoulder to shoulder with the troops. You know everyone who works for you, and even if you don't, rest assured, they know you—sometimes even better than you know yourself!

In a large organization, this same dynamic exists in each department, unit or area.

Once again, compassion and strong lines of communication

are essential to the cultivation of effective leader/follower relationships. Loss of this interpersonal connection can degrade leadership efficacy in any size organization, but in a very small operation you feel the impact immediately and the effects can be crippling.

When you occupy the same physical space as your followers, they see you in a much more intimate way. They can read your moods, they learn your body language, they react to subtle cues. Their performance reflects your demeanor.

Can a leader be both a leader and a friend?

Of course, but that's not completely necessary.

I'm not saying you have to be *friends* with everyone who works for you. I am saying that it's important to *"keep friendship"* with them.

This concept comes from the Student Creed I used in my martial arts centers for years. This creed was a gift from the remarkable martial arts Master and community leader, Jhoon Rhee.

One of the promises in the creed is:

"TO KEEP FRIENDSHIP WITH ONE ANOTHER—TO BUILD A STRONG AND HAPPY COMMUNITY."

You may not spend a lot of personal time with everyone who works for you—you might not ever see most of them outside of work.

On the clock—it serves you well to develop a personal interest and a cordial relationship with each employee in your care.

What this really means, is to treat one another with respect.

It means cultivating an understanding of one another, particularly as it relates to the group and the task at hand.

It means preserving amiable conduct and communication as much as possible to assure a comfortable and productive environment.

This type of openness gives you insights that are not available to the manager who shuts himself in the office. You'll pick up on subtle changes that alert you to trouble or allow you to recognize innovation and outstanding efforts in real time.

This openness builds trust and loyalty with your employees—the people who willingly dedicate their time and talents to help you realize your vision.

It serves you well to appreciate the impact that your personal interest and involvement means to the people working for you. Study after study shows that one of the prime motivators for any employee is the sincere appreciation and personal interest of a supervisor.

If you own a very small business, you may be the only formally recognized supervisor.

Your attention means something!

ESSENTIAL CONDITIONS

First let's cover the essential conditions needed to cultivate leaders at all levels.

There are two:

1-MAKE SURE PEOPLE UNDERSTAND THE LEVEL OF AUTONOMY AND DISCRETION APPROPRIATE TO THEIR ROLES.

2-CULTIVATE AND SUPPORT AUTONOMY WITH CONTINUAL TRAINING AND BY SUPPORTING YOUR PEOPLE WHEN THEY ACT INDEPENDENTLY.

This is why I place such an emphasis on continual leadership training and development.

If you want people to have the capacity to act independently, to be leaders—you have to support them with the training they need to grow and develop as people and as leaders.

It also means standing with them when mistakes are made.

Of course you don't want people making foolish mistakes—and the worst is making the same foolish mistake twice. If people are not meeting your standards after giving them sufficient opportunity, then changes must be made.

However, when someone is genuinely acting in your best interests and the results are not immediately favorable, you've got to support their decision or action—even if you decide that a different course is necessary next time. That's the only way to encourage individual creativity and assure an innovative culture.

As Confucius said:

"THE CAUTIOUS SELDOM ERR."

Cautious people seldom send men to the moon either!

As a leader, it's your job to create the conditions that allow people to perform effectively on their own—the very definition of power.

ESSENTIAL ORGANIZATION CONDITIONS

No matter what the size of your organization, these conditions are essential:

OPEN LINES OF COMMUNICATION

CLEARLY DEFINED AND ARTICULATED EXPECTATIONS, MISSION AND PURPOSE

CONSISTENCY IN YOUR TREATMENT OF THE PEOPLE ON THE FRONT LINES— FAIRNESS

PERSONAL MENTORING & GUIDANCE— FROM YOU!

People in large organizations recoil at the thought of having to navigate political channels or negotiate various levels to get the support and guidance they want and need.

It's even worse in a small business where your employees see you, *in person,* every single day.

Make yourself accessible and available. Make sure when you say your door is always open, it actually is.

I often play a *"Stump the Black Belt"* game in my presentations. People in the audience can ask me just about anything about leadership, business or life—and I answer their questions from my perspective as a Black Belt and Sensei.

If you stump me, you get a signed book.

I did this exercise at a CEO Club event in Baltimore. Instead of asking a question, Bill, the CEO of a very successful small company, started telling a story ...

Bill told us about his commitment to personal contact with everyone in his company. He told us about his authentic open-door policy.

He said he routinely comes in early, stays late, and does whatever it takes to address the needs of his employees, both professionally and, to the best of his ability, personally.

I could tell he thought he had me stumped when he said:

"Some people say I'm too personal with my employees. What have you got to say about that?"

I just walked over, dropped a book on his table and said:

"You sir—think like a Black Belt!"

Bill is the embodiment of The Sensei Leader.

LEADERS VS. MANAGERS: WHAT'S THE DIFFERENCE?

> "MANAGEMENT IS EFFICIENCY IN
> CLIMBING THE LADDER OF SUCCESS;
> LEADERSHIP DETERMINES WHETHER
> THE LADDER IS LEANING AGAINST
> THE RIGHT WALL."
>
> ~STEPHEN COVEY

Whenever I want to start a fight at one of my events, all I have to do is talk about leadership at all levels. There are two distinct perspectives:

First—there are those who respond aggressively. They cry, "Too many chiefs!"

You just can't have everyone giving orders and nobody carrying them out. *Right?*

True.

Then—there are those who understand that "leadership" is not a quality restricted to conventional "leaders," that it's not limited to the people who have command and control.

To embrace and fully exploit the potential of leadership at all levels, you've got to make a clear distinction between leadership and management.

Earlier I quoted a definition of leadership by John Quincy Adams. This is a concept worthy of repetition:

"IF YOUR ACTIONS INSPIRE OTHERS TO DREAM MORE, LEARN MORE, DO MORE AND BECOME MORE, YOU ARE A LEADER."

Adams says nothing about title, rank or position.

Was Rosa Parks a leader? She held no formal position of authority. She wasn't a corporate executive or a pastor—she was a seamstress.

She was an ordinary person who answered the call and through her actions she inspired generations of people to continue the fight for social justice.

Was Einstein a leader? He didn't seem to think so, and he was well known for his ability to think!

Einstein purposely avoided positions of authority, yet he inspired a new age of learning, thinking and progress in science and humanity.

Leaders have always emerged from all levels. Leadership

is your ability and willingness to be an example to others. It's your ability to inspire and your willingness to help others achieve by sharing your wisdom and experience—and by sharing yourself.

Management is a different issue. There is a vast difference between the *leader* and the *boss*.

Teddy Roosevelt had an interesting perspective …

> ## "PEOPLE ASK THE DIFFERENCE BETWEEN A LEADER AND A BOSS. THE LEADER LEADS, AND THE BOSS DRIVES."

Seems simple enough to understand, but I also like the way Peter Drucker expresses it:

> ## "MANAGEMENT IS DOING THINGS RIGHT; LEADERSHIP IS DOING THE RIGHT THINGS."

In these simple statements you can see that leadership transcends management. Leadership operates on a higher dimension than command and control.

It's simple, really.

Management denotes a position of authority.

Leadership is independent of authority.

Leadership implies a sincere commitment to ethical and

moral excellence. A leader is someone whose very life, expressed through words and action, provides an example for others.

You can be a leader without holding an official position of authority—but it's very difficult to maintain a position of authority without being an effective leader.

If you are a manager or anyone else in a position of authority, the transcendent qualities of leadership help you earn the trust and loyalty of the people who carry out your orders and work with you to get the job done. That's what gives you the capacity to lead effectively—your power as a leader.

Many experts preach that a leader has no power without authority. I see exactly the opposite.

A leader has no authority without power—not for long anyway!

The more effective you are, the greater the positive impact you have on the lives of the people who follow you willingly, the more likely those people are to trust, invest in and support your authority.

That's true power.

On the other hand, someone can be vested with a tremendous amount of authority without the capacity to act effectively—without the ability to perform in any meaningful way.

That's the very definition of the proverbial "empty suit."

Here's another helpful observation from John W. Gardner:

> One reason corporate and governmental bureaucracies
> stagnate is the assumption by line executives that
> given their rank and authority, they can lead without
> being leaders. They cannot. They can be given sub-
> ordinates, but they cannot be given a following.

A following must be earned.

In the same way, The Sensei must earn the authority vested in him by his students.

There are plenty of talented martial artists that make lousy
teachers. There are also plenty of talented managers, bureau-
crats and administrators that make lousy leaders.

There is an epidemic of people infecting positions of authority who may have outstanding domain knowledge or
even a record of high performance in other positions, but still
just don't have what it takes to be a true leader.

That's exactly what fuels the tired debate over leadership
versus management.

Managerial skills are by nature more technical and func-
tionary. You need those skills to manage process.

Leadership skills are those that make you more effective in
your relationships with people.

Management always refers to a position of authority—a title. A title or position is almost always conferred by superiors

or advisors and may or may not involve input from subordinates or followers.

You can also establish authority simply by acquiring a title and convincing others that you know more than they do. You can dictate a strict culture full of perfunctory rituals that reinforce your authority, status and position. You can increase authority through political maneuvering, lying and cheating.

You can even attain a position of authority by being a jerk!

Authentic leadership, on the other hand, is always dependent on acknowledgement from subordinates and peers.

No followers—no leader!

Authority is always limited by the willingness of the people under you to share their talents and abilities.

A manager may have the authority to dictate the performance of certain tasks. It takes a genuine leader to inspire the best performance in others.

Dwight D. Eisenhower sums it all up quite neatly:

"LEADERSHIP IS THE ART OF GETTING SOMEONE ELSE TO DO SOMETHING YOU WANT DONE BECAUSE HE WANTS TO DO IT."

You may express leadership from a position of authority

as a manager, boss, commander or executive. You may also express leadership peer to peer or up the ranks as well as down.

You can't always share authority, and sometimes you shouldn't.

Leadership can and should always be shared—at all levels.

Leadership is not only possible at all levels, leadership is your responsibility ...

... At all levels.

主
領

Do these 3 things...

"Before I studied the art, a punch to me was just like a punch, a kick just like a kick. After I learned the art, a punch was no longer a punch, a kick no longer a kick. Now that I've understood the art, a punch is just like a punch, a kick just like a kick."

~Bruce Lee

Years ago I thought the Masters were trying to be wiseasses with these mystical rants. Now I understand.

As tough as it was to earn a Black Belt, my transformation as a person and a leader was even tougher.

I experienced plenty of moments when I seriously questioned whether I was worthy to lead anybody—plenty of times when I didn't think I was doing a very good job leading my own life.

During many of those moments, it seemed to me that the experience of leadership was just overwhelming—too complex. I couldn't seem to grasp the nuances.

Over 30 years of practice, I started to make some sense of it. I don't believe I know it all—but I am now confident about what I do know and understand.

BEFORE I STUDIED LEADERSHIP, A LEADER WAS JUST A LEADER.

AFTER I LEARNED A LITTLE ABOUT LEADERSHIP, A LEADER WAS NO LONGER A LEADER—AND I CERTAINLY WASN'T SURE I COULD BE ONE.

NOW THAT I KNOW SOMETHING ABOUT LEADERSHIP, A LEADER IS JUST A LEADER—AND JUST A PERSON TRYING TO DO HIS BEST.

If not easier, it does seem simpler now. I believe we have a tendency to over-complicate leadership.

With the benefit of experience, everything I've learned about leadership can be reduced to these 3 simple steps:

LISTEN MORE ...

LEARN MORE ...

FEAR LESS.

LISTEN MORE

How many studies and reports do we need before we finally acknowledge what already exists?

People want leaders who are connected, who understand what's happening on the front lines, and who truly care about the people under their responsibility.

They want leaders who listen!

One of the top reasons always cited for disengagement is disconnected or unresponsive leadership. People choose to follow you because your vision supports and works in harmony with theirs.

Leaders who listen, pay attention and focus on the needs, goals and motivations of the people in their organizations are outperforming the competition by miles.

LEARN MORE

I said this earlier, but it might stick a little better if I show it in the form of a pithy quote:

PEOPLE FOLLOW EXAMPLES MUCH MORE ENTHUSIASTICALLY THAN ORDERS.

Simple—not easy. Model the behavior you expect from others.

You must lead by example, especially in your continual pursuit of personal and professional excellence. Commit yourself to continual learning, growth and development—if you expect others to do the same.

The world and the business environment is changing at an ever accelerating pace. Your success depends upon your ability to learn faster, or at least as fast, as your competition.

It's no longer good enough to keep up—you've got to lead from the front!

Keep your sword sharp. Show your followers that you're always willing to learn more ...

... especially from them.

FEAR LESS

I'm sure you know by now that I have nothing against fear. Fear only becomes a problem when we allow fear to stop us from doing something important or meaningful.

As we've said again and again, courageous people are those who face their fears and do what needs to be done anyway.

Some leaders act as if they're fearless. I'll paraphrase General Patton once more: *people without fear are not brave, they're idiots!*

Seemingly fearless people are either psychotic—or they're just too ignorant to know what they're getting into! People are much more likely to follow you when they see you face your fears and act with courage.

Don't aspire to be fearless—simply fear less.

A leader's job is not easy, but it is simple ...

LISTEN MORE ...

LEARN MORE ...

FEAR LESS.

主
領

THE SPIRIT OF THE LEADER

"ENLIGHTENED LEADERSHIP IS SPIRITUAL
IF WE UNDERSTAND SPIRITUALITY NOT
AS SOME KIND OF RELIGIOUS DOGMA
OR IDEOLOGY BUT AS THE DOMAIN OF
AWARENESS WHERE WE EXPERIENCE
VALUES LIKE TRUTH, GOODNESS,
BEAUTY, LOVE AND COMPASSION, AND
ALSO INTUITION, CREATIVITY, INSIGHT
AND FOCUSED ATTENTION."

~DEEPAK CHOPRA

Before you think I'm going all new-age on you, hear me out!

In martial arts, we talk a lot about body, mind and spirit. These are the sources of human power: your capacity to perform effectively as a human being and as a leader.

Do you remember how I defined success earlier?

I defined success as a sense of abundance in three major areas: *material, emotional* and *spiritual*. These are the resources you must cultivate and nourish in order to live a happy, productive and successful life.

You could say that success is the ultimate objective of the leader. The leader's primary responsibility is the success of the group—the organization, family or community.

Warren Bennis said it this way:

"LEADERSHIP IS THE CAPACITY TO TRANSLATE VISION INTO REALITY."

Your success as a leader is defined by your ability to transform something *intangible*, your vision, into something *real*— by leading the efforts of others.

When martial artists talk about spiritual resources, we're talking exactly about those intangible characteristics, qualities and values that are difficult if not impossible to measure or quantify.

We're talking about feelings.

Courage is a great example of a spiritual resource …

Courage only becomes tangible through action—when you act courageously under pressure. Until then, courage is just a possibility—an expectation—a feeling.

Courage is a capacity.

Think about it this way: you can't *see* courage any more than you can *see* the voltage stored in a battery. You can only observe a human being acting courageously, as an action—just as you can only see the effects of electricity when you turn on the switch and the light comes on.

Leadership works the same way …

Leadership is a capacity.

Your capacity for leadership is contained in your potential to inspire, teach, motivate and care for others.

You can only experience leadership through action—through your expression of courage, compassion and wisdom and through your interactions with the people who are willing to follow you.

Another vital spiritual commodity is the sense of purpose and meaning I've been trumpeting throughout this book.

Purpose and meaning are *feelings.*

Any measurement of them is subjective and their presence or relative intensity is a matter of personal opinion and perspective.

Still, I dare you to try and find any competent leader who doubts how important a sense of purpose is to the success of the organization—or the individual.

In *Principle Centered Leadership,* Stephen R. Covey wrote:

> We see that people are not just resources or assets, not just economic, social and psychological beings. They are also spiritual beings; they want meaning, a sense of doing something that matters ... There must be purposes that lift them, and bring them to their highest selves.

Give THAT man a Black Belt!

People do not perform to their highest potential unless their material and emotional needs are satisfied, and unless they are given the opportunity to explore their spiritual ambitions—their sense of purpose.

Material needs are important, too, but only to a degree.

Research today clearly indicates that material incentives are only effective relative to fairly mundane tasks. Work that requires a higher level of intellectual engagement also requires a higher degree of emotional and spiritual incentive.

This research also shows a point of diminishing returns when it comes to material rewards.

People respond well to monetary rewards up to a point, but once basic material needs are satisfied, performance only increases significantly in proportion to other motivators, and three of the strongest are autonomy, mastery and purpose.

The most spiritual aspect of leadership is your ability to connect with other human beings.

To me—this sense of connection to others defines what we

experience as *spiritual*. Your desire to serve a purpose above and beyond your own self-interest defines your spirit as a leader.

Human beings simply cannot live successfully in isolation. Sure, the occasional master would crawl off to a cave to live as a hermit once in a while, but not to escape. Their isolation was meant to turn off the noise, gain perspective, and search for the way for us to live more connected, meaningful lives.

The genuine leader is committed to the satisfaction of our need to be connected, to work cooperatively, to belong and to serve a greater purpose.

The effective leader cultivates these desires, focuses the group on the pursuit of a meaningful objective and, most of all, inspires the highest levels of performance by supporting each individual's instinctive need to matter.

I've learned that leadership is not about telling people what to do—it's about seeing what needs to be done and calling people to do it along with you.

It's about living as a model of the expectations you have for others. That doesn't mean you're perfect, it means you are constantly perfecting. It doesn't mean you do everything right, it means you're always moving in the right direction.

Leadership also means that you can't carry everyone up the mountain. Your mission is to guide people to the summit.

Sometimes you're on the point; sometimes you're climbing in support.

Spirituality is about reaching outside your Self.

It's literally about embracing and nurturing the human spirit, yours and that of the people who recognize you as a leader, and directing that collective spirit for the benefit of all.

Nobody embodies this type of leadership more than a teacher—a Sensei. A teacher's calling is to share and steward the most precious human resource: potential.

Through my transformation from loser to leader, I learned that the warrior is only tested by the mettle of his opponent.

I learned that my toughest opponent is the person I see in my bathroom mirror each and every morning.

Now I also know that my followers are my best mirror. Their accomplishments serve as my most accurate reflection as a leader.

Ultimately—a teacher is a guide through the never-ending process of transformation, and that is truly a spiritual experience.

When you truly lead by example, you are always engaged in the natural cycle of transformation. This cycle is as critical to an organization as it is to an individual.

The leader's role is to inspire and engage others in that process.

If you want to find your true spirit—your true potential to make a difference in the world—then make a difference in the lives of the people around you.

BE THE SENSEI.

BE THE LEADER.

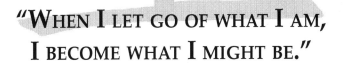

"WHEN I LET GO OF WHAT I AM,
I BECOME WHAT I MIGHT BE."

~LAO TZU

RESOURCES

In my ongoing search to be a better leader, I've read literally hundreds of useful books and countless articles in journals, periodicals and online.

Rather than a traditional bibliography limited to the resources cited in the book, I decided to share a few of what I've found to be the most useful and informative materials that helped me grow as a leader.

I'd like to extend special thanks to J. Thomas Wren for his incredible book, *The Leader's Companion: Insights on Leadership Through the Ages.*

Dr. Wren is a noted scholar and author of several books on leadership. He is also Professor Emeritus at the Jepson School of Leadership Studies.

The Leader's Companion is a compilation of some of the most insightful leadership writing available, from Lao Tzu to today's leading thinkers.

Dr. Wren's book saved me countless hours of research time—*The Leader's Companion* belongs on every leader's shelf!

BOOKS ON LEADERS

Here you'll find biographies, autobiographies and studies on notable leaders, past and present:

- *American Soldier*   General Tommy Franks
- *The Autobiography of Malcolm X*
- *Bayonet! Forward!*   Joshua L. Chamberlain
- *The Education of a Coach*   David Halberstam
- *Einstein: His Life and Universe* Walter Isaacson
- *Freedom in Exile*   H.H. The Dalai Lama
- *A Pride of Lions*   William Lemke
- *The First American: The Life and Times of Benjamin Franklin*
    H. W. Brands
- *First Man: The Life of Neil A. Armstrong*
    James R. Hansen

JIM BOUCHARD

- *Franklin: Autobiography and Other Writings*
  Oxford Classics
- *Founding Brothers: The Revolutionary Generation*
  Joseph J. Ellis
- *General Patton: A Soldier's Life* Stanley P. Hirsham
- *Joshua Chamberlain: A Hero's Life and Legacy*
  John J. Pullen
- *The Last Coach: A Life of Paul "Bear" Bryant*
  Robert Allen Barra
- *Leadership*   Rudolph W. Giuliani
- *Lee*   Douglas Southall Freeman
- *Lincoln on Leadership*   Donald T. Phillips
- *Martin Luther King, Jr., On Leadership*
  Donald T. Phillips
- *May I Quote You, General Chamberlain?*
  Edited by Randall Bedwell
- *The Measure of a Man*   Sydney Poitier
- *Mountbatten*   Richard Hough
- *Nothing Stood in Her Way*   Julie Clark
- *Patton on Leadership*   Alan Axelrod
- *Personal Memoirs of U.S. Grant*
- *A Soldier's Story*   Omar N. Bradley
- *Soul of The Lion*   William M. Wallace
- *Unbroken*   Laura Hillenbrand
- *War As I Knew It*   General George S. Patton
- *The Victors: Eisenhower and His Boys*
  Stephen A. Ambrose

BOOKS ON LEADERSHIP

These are books specifically focused on styles, process, techniques, and theories of leadership:

- *Be the Best at What Matters Most*
  Joe Calloway
- *Carrots and Sticks Don't Work* Paul Marciano
- *Fiercely Loyal* Dov Baron
- *It's Your Ship* Michael Abrashoff
- *The Leader's Companion* J. Thomas Wren
- *Leadership* James MacGregor Burns
- *~~...~~rship by Virtue* Jaro Berce
- *No-Compromise Leadership* Neil Ducoff
- *Principle Centered Leadership* Stephen R. Covey
- *Start With Why* Simon Sinek

ETHICS

Books on how to do the right thing—even when it's tough:

- *The Cost of Bad Behavior* Christine Pearson & Christine Porath
- *Grow A Pair* Larry Winget
- *Ethics for a New Millennium* H.H. The Dalai Lama
- *Ethics: The Essential Writings* Edited by Gordon Marino
- *How Good People Make Tough Choices*
  Rushworth M. Kidder
- *In Search of Ethics* Len Marrella
- *Moral Courage* Rushworth M. Kidder
- *Moral Minds* Marc D. Hauser
- *The Tao of Power* R. L. Wing
- *Zorba the Greek* Nikos Kazantzakis

MARTIAL ARTS AND PHILOSOPHY

Martial arts and Eastern philosophy has greatly informed my view of leadership. Here are some of my favorites, including books on martial technique you can apply to leadership—whether you kick or punch—or not:

- *The Analects*   Confucius
- *The Art of War*   Sun Tzu,
                                    Translated by Thomas Cleary
- *The Bodhisattva Warriors*   Shifu Nagaboshi Tomio
- *Code of the Samurai*   Translated by Thomas Cleary
- *Chinese Martial Arts Manuals: A Historical Survey*
                                    Brian Kennedy
                                    & Elizabeth Guo
- *Comprehensive Applications of Shaolin Chin Na*
                                    Dr. Yang Jwing-Ming
- *Hagakure: The Book of the Samurai*
                                    Yamamoto Tsunetomo
- *In Search of Kenpo*   James Mitose
- *Living the Martial Way*   Forrest E. Morgan
- *Miyamoto Musashi: His Life and Writings*
                                    Kenji Tokitsu
- *The Overlook Martial Arts Reader*
                                    Randy F. Nelson
- *The Ring of the Way*   Taisen Deshimaru
- *The Search for Inner Strength*   Chuck Norris
- *Steal My Art: The Life and Times of Taiji Master T.T. Liang*
                                    Stuart Alve Olson
- *Sun Tzu for Success*   Gerald Michaelson
- *Tai-Chi*   Cheng Man-ch'ing
                                    & Robert W. Smith
- *Tai Chi Classics*   Translated by Waysun Liao

- *Tai Chi Secrets of the Ancient Masters*
  Dr. Yang Jwing-Ming
- *The Tao of Jeet Kune Do*   Bruce Lee
- *The Tao of the Tao Te Ching*   Michael LaFargue
- *What Is Tao?*   Alan Watts
- *The Way of the Warrior*   Howard Reid
  & Michael Croucher
- *Zen Flesh, Zen Bones*   Paul Repps

AND MORE ...

Other writings on history, philosophy and other topics that I've found helpful in my development as a leader:

- *Brain Rules*   John Medina
- *Common Sense, Rights of Man and other Essential Writings of Thomas Paine*
- *The Great American Speeches*   Quercus Publishing
- *A History of Knowledge*   Charles Van Doren
- *How to Win Friends and Influence People*
  Dale Carnegie
- *The Law of Success*   Napoleon Hill
- *Mastery*   Robert Greene
- *The Power of Habit*   Charles Duhigg
- *The Power of Myth*   Joseph Campbell
- *The 7 Habits of Highly Effective People*
  Stephen R. Covey
- *A Short History of Nearly Everything*
  Bill Bryson
- *Speeches that Changed the World*
  Smith-Davies Publishing
- *Talent is Overrated*   Geoff Colvin
- *A World of Ideas*   Bill Moyers

OTHER RESOURCES

In addition, I'd like to acknowledge some of the journals and online resources I depend for data, news, current issues, and to deepen my understanding of leadership:

- *Fast Company & FastCompany.com*
- *Forbes.com*
- *Gallup.com*
- *Harvard Business Review & HBR.org*
- *McKinsey Quarterly & McKinsey.com/insights*
- *Scientific American Mind*

And a special thanks to BrainyQuote.com!

GRATITUDE

It's always a blessing to give thanks to the people who make a book possible. I want to express my gratitude to a few special people who were instrumental in helping me through one more major transformation.

Ian Smith and Lynsie Hall—I wish I could express how much your validation meant to me in the early stages of this project. I never occupied the corner office; it is validating to know that what I'm doing means something to the people who do!

Alonzo Meyers—you're right, there is no bond like that between brothers of the Greatest Game. Thank You for your continued friendship and support, my brother.

Steve Wallace—you are the model leader in my opinion! Your belief in my work is greatly appreciated. Your friendship is treasured.

William E. Sergiy—If you're lucky enough to survive, you realize that a few very special people are the rocks upon which you build your life. I'm that lucky and you're one of those people!
Thanks Old Sensei!

Dave Melville—every time I need you, there you are! By the way, I pledge not to say *"I don't want to jinx it"* ever again.

Tam Veilleux and Real Castonguay—Your encouragement and belief was a constant source of energy. Your friendship is a blessing and your indefatigable positivity is a continual presence!

Ed and Linda Pritchard—Your belief in this work was empowering. I cannot tell you much it means to both Alex and me to part of your family. *Now—let's go see those little horses!*

Larry Winget and Joe Calloway—I wanted to thank you together, because together you changed the course of our lives. You've become trusted mentors and treasured friends. Your generosity, encouragement and enthusiasm have been an important part of this journey.

You've brought out the best in me in this business so far, and your advice and wisdom is a beacon to me every day.

You are both **Sensei** *in every sense of the word.*

Every fighter needs great people in his corner.

I am fortunate and grateful to have all of you in mine.

Thank You!

Also the author of THINK Like a BLACK BELT— *Jim Bouchard tours nationally teaching personal and professional Mastery and Leadership for corporate and conference audiences.*

He is a frequent guest on TV and radio programs including *FOX News Live, BBC Worldview* and *FOX Across America.*

Jim is the founder of Northern Chi Martial Arts Center where he still serves as Master Instructor in Residence.

An obsessive golfer, Jim lives in Brunswick, Maine with his wife and business partner, Alex.

THESENSEILEADER.COM
THATBLACKBELTGUY.COM

FOR BOOKING:
BLACK BELT MINDSET PRODUCTIONS
800.786.8502

20200724R00197

Made in the USA
Middletown, DE
19 May 2015